EDITOR: MARTIN WIND

OSPREY MILITARY

MEN-AT-ARMS SERIES

222

THE AGE OF TAMERLANE

Text by
DAVID NICOLLE PhD
Colour plates by
ANGUS McBRIDE

First published in Great Britain in 1990 by
Osprey Publishing, Elms Court, Chapel Way,
Botley, Oxford OX2 9LP, United Kingdom.
Email: osprey@osprey-publishing.co.uk
© Copyright 1990 Osprey Publishing Ltd
Reprinted 1991, 1995, 1996, 1999

British Library Cataloguing in Publication Data
Nicolle, David *1944–*
    The age of Tamerlane. — (Men-at-arms series; 222)
    1. Mongol Empire. Tamerlane
    I. Title   II. McBride, Angus
    950.2092

    ISBN 0-85045-949-4

Filmset in Great Britain
Printed through World Print Ltd, Hong Kong

FOR A CATALOGUE OF ALL BOOKS PUBLISHED BY
OSPREY MILITARY, AUTOMOTIVE AND AVIATION
PLEASE WRITE TO:

The Marketing Manager, Osprey Publishing, PO
Box 140, Wellingborough, Northants, NN8 4ZA,
United Kingdom

VISIT OSPREY'S WEBSITE AT:

http://www.osprey-publishing.co.uk

Dedication
For Colette, too sweet for a Tartar

Artist's Note
Readers may care to note that the original paintings
from which the colour plates in this book were
prepared are available for private sale. All
reproduction copyright whatsoever is retained by the
Publishers. All enquiries should be addressed to:
    Scorpio
    PO Box 475,
    Hailsham,
    E. Sussex BN27 2SL
The Publishers regret that they can enter into no
correspondence upon this matter.

The Lame Conqueror

Tamerlane or Tamburlane, as he was known in various parts of Europe, is one of the most extraordinary conquerors in history. Within half a lifetime his armies seized huge territories from the borders of Mongolia to Palestine and Anatolia. Mighty states accepted—at least nominally—Timur's overlordship as they cowered before his apparently irresistible armies. His passage was also marked by massacres that outdid even those of the Mongols for sheer savagery. Small wonder that the fame of this complex and nightmarish character spread into Europe, where Timur became the subject not only of Christopher Marlowe's famous play *Tamberlaine the Great* but also of works by Spanish, French and other English writers as well as German, Italian and Czech composers.

The real Tamerlane, or Timur-i-Lenk—('Timur the Lame')—came from a family of Turcified Mongol aristocrats, the Barlas clan. They dominated a small territory south of Samarqand, and owed allegiance to the Mongol Jagatai Khans who had ruled much of Central Asia following the fragmentation of Genghis Khan's Empire in the late 13th century. Timur, whose name means 'iron one', eventually won the titles 'Unconquered Lord of the Seven Climates' and Sahib Qiran ('Lord of the Fortunate Celestial Conjunction'). He had already gained the nickname 'Lame' after being struck by several arrows during a minor skirmish in 1363: one hit Timur in the right leg, another in the right arm, permanently damaging both. (These wounds were confirmed when Timur's tomb was opened by Soviet archaeologists in 1941.) At around the same time Timur was also wounded in the right hand—by his own father's sabre, according to one story.

Timur's astonishing life could fill the pages of several Men-at-Arms books; and the story of the dynasty he established is full of drama, victories and defeats at the hands of various foes including the colourful Qara and Aq Qoyunlu ('Black' and 'White Sheep') Turcomans. Below is a brief chronology of the war-torn years from around Timur's birth to his dynasty's collapse in the early years of the 16th century.

1335	Death of last descendant of Hulegu, start of collapse of Il-Khan (Mongol) authority in Iran.
1336	*Birth of Timur near Kish.*
1368	Yuan (Mongol) dynasty driven out of China by Ming.
1370	*Timur becomes ruler of Transoxania.*
1371	*Timur invades Khwarazm.*
1375–76	*Timur invades Jagatai territory as far as Mongolia.*
1377	Birth of Timur's son Shahrukh.
1377–78	Traditional establishment of Turcoman Qara Qoyunlu and Aq Qoyunlu dynasties in Kurdistan, Armenia and Azarbayjan under Jalayrid suzereinty.

The warriors of 14th C. Iran wore many types of armour. In this Persian manuscript from Shiraz at least four horsemen have mail hauberks while the horse in the centre is protected by lamellar armour and a rigid *chamfron* on its head. (*Kitab-i-Samak Ayyar*, c.1335 AD, Bodleian Lib., Ms. Ous. 381, f.39v, Oxford)

1378	Toqtamish becomes ruler of the Golden Horde.	**1405**	*Death of Timur.*
1380	Prince of Moscow defeats Golden Horde army at battle of Kulikovo Field.	**1406–10**	Revival of Qara Qoyunlu power in eastern Anatolia and defeat of Timurid governors.
1381–84	*Timur invades Afghanistan and eastern Iran, captures Herat.*	**1409**	Shahrukh seizes Samarqand.
1385–88	*Timur invades western Iran, captures Tabriz.*	**1410–11**	Defeat of Jalayrids of Iraq by Qara Qoyunlu.
1387	*Timur captures Isfahan and Shiraz.*	**1412**	Qara Qoyunlu defeat Timurid allies at battle of Kur River.
1391–92	*Timur invades Golden Horde, defeats Toqtamish at battle of Kunduzcha.*	**1413**	Shahrukh's expedition into western Iran and against Qara Qoyunlu.
1392–96	*Timur invades western Iran, Iraq, Georgia, Golden Horde, seizes Baghdad for first time.*	**1421**	Shahrukh defeats Qara Qoyunlu at three-day battle of Alashgird.
1396	Ottoman Sultan Bayazit defeats Crusaders at battle of Nicopolis.	**1423–7**	Wars between Timurid Ulugh Beg and Mongols, defeat of Ulugh Beg.
1398–99	*Timur invades India, defeats Sultan of Delhi at battle of Delhi.*	**1427–36**	Periodic Uzbeg raids from north into Timurid Khwarazm.
1399–1404	*Timur invades Anatolia, Syria, Georgia, defeats Mamluks, captures Aleppo and Damascus, seizes Baghdad for second time, defeats Ottoman Sultan Bayazit at battle of Ankara.*	**1446**	Shahrukh's expedition into western Iran against Qara Qoyunlu; Timurids lose Khwarazm and northern Transoxania to Uzbegs.

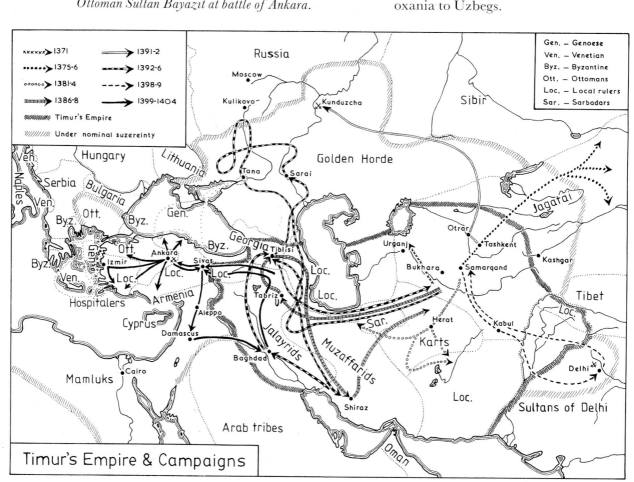

Timur's Empire & Campaigns

1447	Death of Shahrukh.
1447–49	Timurid civil wars.
1449	Murder of Ulugh Beg.
1451	Uzbegs involved in Timurid civil wars.
1453	Ottoman capture of Istanbul (Byzantine Constantinople).
1468	Aq Qoyunlu defeat Timurid Sultan Abu Sa'id.
1469	Turcoman Qara Qoyunlu overthrown by Turcoman Aq Qoyunlu in Armenia, western Iran, Iraq.
1480	Prince of Moscow defeats Golden Horde army at battle of Ugra River, effective liberation of Russia from Mongol domination.
1494–1500	Anarchy in Transoxania, collapse and fragmentation of Timurid power.
1502	Defeat of Turcoman Aq Qoyunlu by Persian Safavids at battle of Shurur, collapse of Aq Qoyunlu.
1503–07	Timurid Prince Babar conquers Afghanistan.
1506	Death of Timurid Sultan Husayn Bayqara of Khurasan, effective end of Timurid dynasty.
1525–26	Timurid Babar of Afghanistan conquers northern India, creation of Mogul dynasty which lasts until British Raj in 1857.

Timur's World

Timur was fortunate, not only in the Celestial Conjunction of stars at his birth but also in the political and military circumstances in which he grew up. The 14th century was a time of turmoil and war in the Muslim world as it was in Europe. The Black Death had ravaged the area, weakening once mighty states like the Mongol Golden Horde north of the Caspian Sea. Less is known about the plague in Iran and the Arab areas but it certainly contributed to instability, decimated the population, hit trade and undermined the semi-feudal structure which maintained not only governments but also armies. Muslim reaction to the Black Death differed from that in Europe. Instead of outbursts of religious hysteria, urban unrest or revolution, the Muslim peoples relied on traditional family or tribal loyalties, reduced their birthrate and hoped for better times. Agriculture retreated as the population slumped. Huge areas reverted to nomadism, while some isolated groups like the Arab bedouin may actually have escaped the plagues relatively lightly. In Europe there was a rapid economic recovery but the Middle East stagnated after the Black Death which, of course, returned in a series of lesser epidemics during what some historians have called the 'Golden Age of Bacteria'...

The fullest evidence comes from Egypt and Syria, where the Mamluk military elite at first escaped the worst ravages of the Black Death but suffered along with everyone else in subsequent epidemics. The revenues from their *iqta* estates fell, as did their standards of military discipline.

The panels in this manuscript made in Shiraz, 1341 AD, show musical instruments, animals and various types of weapon. These include a trident similar to the Italian *ronco*, a straight sword, probably a mace and what could be the arrow-guide from a *nawak*. This device turned an ordinary bow into a temporary crossbow. (*Munis al Ahrar*, Museum of Art, inv. 45.385, Cleveland)

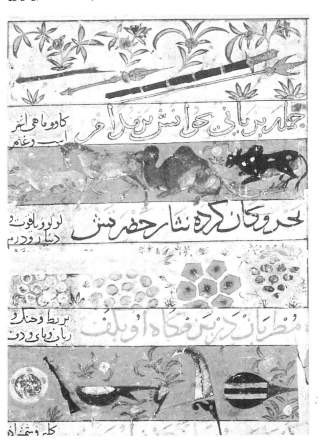

This relatively crude illustration from south-western Iran was made during Timur's life and includes interesting details. Perhaps the most important are laces which secure the turbaned man's lamellar tassets to his legs. (*Shahnamah*, 1371 AD, Topkapi Lib., Ms. Haz. 1511, f.105r, Istanbul)

Because the Mamluks were recruited from slaves, largely brought in from southern Russia, Egypt's military elite was able to maintain its numbers. Elsewhere the freeborn elites of Iran, Iraq and Turkey may have declined both in numbers and military quality.

Timur's homeland of Transoxania did not escape the Black Death, but here the situation was more complicated. The steppe Mongols had reverted to their traditional nomadic ways following the break-up of Genghis Khan's Empire. In the western and central steppes they were now largely Turcified in speech and customs. Even where they retained a distinct identity the Mongols of the Jagatai Kkanate were few in number and mixed in origin. In fact the Jagatai Khanate consisted of two dissimilar regions: Transoxania in the west and Moghulistan or the 'Land of the Mongols' to the east. Moghulistan was largely nomadic with few towns and little agriculture. The Muslim faith was spreading but was as yet so superficial that the people were regarded as being outside the Muslim world by the urbanized, agricultural and deeply Muslim inhabitants of Transoxania. Here, in the western part of the Jagatai Khanate, a Mongol elite still dominated the country but was rapidly losing control over the cities and even the fertile river valleys. Meanwhile the spread of dubious 'folk Islam' practices led the more orthodox Muslim peoples of Iran and the Middle East to doubt whether the Transoxanians were still really Muslim.

The mid-14th century had been a chaotic period of civil wars within the Jagatai Khanate, during which the once flourishing Nestorian Christian communities of Central Asia were obliterated. Paradoxically, however, the cities of Transoxania witnessed a revival of trade and prosperity. Even during Timur's lifetime business was conducted in 'Kebeki' dinars named after Kibak, the last truly effective Jagatai Khan, whose name is still recalled in the *kopek*, the smallest unit of Russian currency.

There does not seem to have been any similar revival in Iran where the Mongol Il-Khan state had collapsed in the mid-14th century. The land which was to fall before Timur's furious assault lay divided between the Karts of the east and the Muzaffarids of the west, both of whom had begun as Mongol vassals. A series of minor dynasties ruled Afghanistan and the Caspian coast, while the Sarbadars held an area south-east of the Caspian. These Sarbadars were an interesting though short-lived dynasty whose name meant 'heads on the gallows'. They arose as Shiite peasant rebels against the last Mongols and were involved in almost constant warfare against their neighbours. These neighbours were in turn united in regarding the Sarbadars as a dangerous threat to an existing order in which the world was dominated by Turks and Mongols—not by Persian peasants!

Further west Iraq and Azarbayjan (north-western Iran) were ruled by the Jalayrid dynasty which, descended from a Mongol tribe, had done much to restore the damage the Mongols had earlier inflicted on Baghdad. To the north, beyond the Caucasus mountains, the Mongol Golden Horde survived but was also falling apart. Nevertheless this Golden Horde kept firm control over the vassal princes of Russia. South of the Caucasus Christian Georgia was expanding towards the Caspian Sea and down into Armenia, an area it contested with Turks, Kurds and even some small Mongol tribes. In Anatolia the Seljuq Sultanate, after surviving the Mongol terror, had collapsed to be replaced by a series of tiny Turkish emirates of whom the Ottomans were but one. As these little states squabbled over the ruins of Seljuq and

Mongol authority, freelance mercenary soldiers and adventurers offered their services to local rulers or fought on their own account, bringing anarchy to town and country alike.

The Genoese not only dominated Black Sea trade but occupied various ports on the north coast of Turkey as well as part of the Crimea in southern Russia, while European Crusaders had seized the rich city of Izmir on the Aegean coast. With hindsight the 14th century is seen as a period of Christian catastrophe in the Near East as the Turks swept into Europe. At the time, however, this was not so obvious—a fact which influenced Christian Europe's attitude to Timur-i-Lenk and his successors.

Timur and his conquests

Timur's career was unequalled since Alexander the Great in terms of constant battlefield success. Only in his youth, while recovering his family estates south of Samarqand, did Timur face occasional defeat. He took on all his neighbours and beat every one. He was undoubtedly a great general yet, unlike Genghis Khan, Timur was no statesman. He led his armies on campaigns whose brutality was unmatched until the 20th century; yet he failed to destroy any of his main foes, despite defeating them in battle. Even more remarkable was the fact that Timur was over 40 years old before setting out to conquer an empire. His energies had previously focused upon seizing and

Some of the manuscripts made in Baghdad shortly before Timur devastated that city show armour in considerable detail. Here a Persian hero's armour is of fine lamellar construction, probably worn over a mail-lined tunic. He also wears metal vambraces to protect his lower arms (*Shahnamah*, c.1390 AD, Topkapi Lib., Ms. Haz. 2153, f.73r, Istanbul)

Before collapsing beneath Timur's repeated invasions, the Jalayrid rulers of Iraq were great patrons of art. This picture of an Iranian hero slaying a *div* or demon was probably made in Baghdad around 1380 AD. The horseman's body armour is hidden beneath his tunic but he has a mail *aventail* hanging from his helmet. (*Shahnamah*, Topkapi Lib., Ms. Haz. 2152, f.48r, Istanbul)

consolidating power in his homeland of Transoxania. Most of Timur's later life was subsequently spent on campaign; yet he remained an inefficient conqueror, constantly returning to face stubborn 'rebels', a thing Genghis Khan rarely had to do.

Timur's aims also differed from those of Genghis Khan. For example, he apparently had no wish to rule the vast but poor steppes of Central Asia and southern Russia. His expeditions to the north or north-east were intended to crush the remaining Jagatai Khans and ensure that the Golden Horde never became a threat to his rear. Even Timur's campaigns in Iran, Iraq, India, Syria, the Caucasus and Anatolia were largely for loot. Booty and the skilled craftsmen whom his troops dragged back to Samarqand were to enrich Timur's homeland. Even where he did establish a permanent administration it generally proved inefficient and short-lived. In fact the effect of Timur's wars, beyond the frontiers of Transoxania itself, was to complete the destruction started by the Mongols and which had been only partially repaired by their successors. He ruined trade and reduced populations by a sometimes staggering amount, though again contemporary chroniclers probably exaggerated the extent of the devastation. Timur might have been a great soldier, but in purely historical terms he could be seen as the greatest bandit of all time. His empire soon fell apart, though his descendants did hold much of eastern Iran and Afghanistan, as well as Transoxania. There, ironically, they ruled over one of the finest flowerings of art and architecture in the history of Islamic civilisation.

Timur despised the Tajiks or Iranian-speaking urban and agricultural population of Transoxania. Unlike the cultured military elites of most of the Muslim world, Timur came from a rough frontier province and was himself virtually uneducated. Yet he was by no means ignorant: he spoke several languages, had a broad knowledge of political and military affairs, and regarded himself as an expert on religious matters. The Mongols, even those who had superficially converted to Islam, still followed their traditional *yasa* or code of tribal law as finalised by Genghis Khan. Timur added the Islamic *sharia* legal code in what might have been a political tactic to win Islamic religious support. Timur also took pains to spare Muslim shrines during his otherwise devastating campaigns, though there were notable exceptions; the venerable Umayyad Great Mosque in Damascus was, for example, burned in what might have been an accident. Timur's own religious feelings are unknown, but he did make a great show of piety, and was eventually buried at the feet of Nur Sayyid Baraka, a saint who had offered him advice throughout much of his life.

Despite such public piety, Timur-i-Lenk re-

One of the finest manuscripts from Baghdad was made by Junayd al Sultani in 1396 AD, between Timur's two seizures of the city. On one page a vanquished warrior wears ordinary lamellar armour over a short-sleeved mail shirt while the victor seems to have an early version of mail-and-plate cuirass. Both of their animals also have horse-armour, that on the right being of large leather lamellae, that on the left of narrow iron lamellae. Another page shows the ancient Persian Emperor Anushirvan. His guards wear typical Timurid hats and carry their ruler's sabre, small shield and bow. (*Three Romances by Khwaju Kirmani*, British Lib., Ms. Add. 18113, London)

tained a typical Mongol love of alcohol in large quantities and his drunkenness became proverbial. Meanwhile, in a transparent attempt to cling to the letter if not the spirit of Islamic law, the only people who were allowed to drink wine at Timur's court were Christians, others being restricted to alternative forms of beverage. Huge amounts of food, as well as drink and women, were 'consumed' at Timur's court with an almost modern dedication to conspicuous consumption. The status of Timurid wives and concubines was remarkably liberated and indeed influential, further offending orthodox Muslim opinion.

Close to the end of his life and during an almost orgiastic wedding feast that preceded his last campaign, the semi-crippled, half-blind Timur still joined in the dancing. Like most such Timurid celebrations, the feast took place in the open air and in tents whose sumptuous decoration amazed western visitors like the Castilian ambassador Ruy Gonzales Clavijo. In fact Timur had a particular love for fine tents and, according to Clavijo, his audience pavilion was square, each side measuring a hundred paces. Its walls were of black, white and yellow silk bands with overhanging porticos supported by pillars. Its tall domed roof was held up by twelve blue, gold and other coloured pillars as thick as a man's body. On top of the dome was a silken turret with battlements, the entire structure being secured by crimson ropes. The interior of this immense tent was lined with red tapestries decorated with eagles at each corner, and inside stood a raised dais where Timur held court. Other royal or princely tents stood around, including one that served as a mosque, all being enclosed by a silken wall with another battlemented portico over its entrance.

In addition to food, drink, song and dance, entertainment at the wedding feast included acrobats, parades of foreign gifts such as ostriches and a giraffe from Egypt, as well as elephant and horse races. Finally Timur issued an edict which permitted all forms of pleasure and, as the unsympathetic chronicler Ahmad Arabshah wrote: 'every suitor hastened to his desire and every lover met his beloved, without anyone harassing another or superior dealing proudly with inferior, whether in the army or among citizens ... nor was the sword drawn except the sword of contemplation, nor the

This illustration from Shiraz, 1397 AD, shows a warrior in a full mail hauberk plus lower arm vambraces including flaps to protect the backs of his hands. His helmet has pendant earflaps laced to its rim as well as a mail *aventail*. (*Shahinshah-namah*, British Lib., Ms. Or. 2780, f.213v, London)

spear brandished except the lances of love that bent by embrace.'

Though Arabshah's hatred of Timur stemmed from his own suffering at the conqueror's hands, he could not help admiring the man. According to Ahmad Arabshah, Timur 'did not love jest or falsehood; wit and sport pleased him not. He was not sad in adversity nor joyful in prosperity. He did not allow in his company any obscene talk or talk of bloodshed or captivity, rape, plunder or violation of the harem. He was spirited and brave and inspired awe and obedience. He loved bold and brave soldiers by whose aid he opened the locks of terror and tore in pieces men like lions and through them and their battles overturned the heights of mountains.'

Timur's Army

Legend has Timur-i-Lenk reduced to one follower in 1362, but in reality he led a mixed army built around a core of faithful Turco-Mongol tribal troops. He probably inherited a small following in his rôle as a member of the feudal elite of Kish near Samarqand. Tribal nomads may have been the most warlike element in Timur's rapidly expanding army, but the feudal aristocracy from settled agricultural areas provided another pillar of support, as did the cities. Among the latter were urban militia forces known as *sarbadars* but, like the similarly named rulers of north-eastern Iran, they proved to be turbulent and potentially revolutionary. Success bred success for Timur, and he was generally able to expand his army before major campaigns.

In a mixed region like Transoxania, on the frontier of Islam, it is not surprising to find different religions as well as ethnic groups represented in Timur's supposedly Muslim army. His enemies probably exaggerated the fact, but pagans, shamanists, Zoroastrians, Christians and others were all found beneath Timur's banner. The army which invaded Anatolia in 1402, for example, included men from Transoxania, the steppes of Turkestan, India and Iran; while the force that set out to invade China in the year of Timur's death had Transoxanians, Jagatai Mongols, Khurasanis, Mazandaranis and Sistanis from Iran, Afghans, Turcomans from Anatolia, Azarbayjanis, Persians from Fars and Iraqis—there were probably Armenians as well. Some of these troops must have had extraordinary stories to tell of such tumultuous times, but few were recorded.

The looming walls of Ankara's Citadel date from many periods. The towers are close set and protrude to provide excellent artillery bastions. Almost within sight of this Citadel Timur routed the Ottoman army in 1402 AD but whereas Timur's Empire proved a short-lived creation, the Ottomans revived to create a state which endured into modern times. (Author's photograph)

The outline of one soldier's life was, however, written down. He came from a cultured rather than tribal or nomadic background, won fame as a noted warrior and also wrote poetry, and in the closing years of his life retired to the desert as a Muslim hermit.

Nomads remained, however, the backbone of Timur's power. Most came from Transoxania, from 40 tribes which claimed Jagatai Mongol origin. Each provided a military contingent according to its size and in return the tribe enjoyed a legally free, tax-exempt status. Such nomad troops were led by their own *aymak* officers and also provided elite units. Military rôles were largely hereditary and one guard unit, the *gautchin*, had a long tradition going back to Mongol times. By Timur's days, in fact, these *gautchin* had almost become a tribe in their own right.

Transoxania still had a largely Iranian-speaking native majority in the 15th century and it was from these Iranians that the turbulent *sarbadar* militias were drawn. They defended Samarqand against the Jagatai Khan's last attempt to retake Transoxania early in Timur's career, for which Timur rewarded them by executing their leaders as 'revolutionaries'. Nevertheless Timur had a high regard for the *sarbadars'* military capabilities, employing those of neighbouring Khurasan as well as those of the Transoxanian cities. Most would, of course, have been infantry skilled in siege warfare.

The vast crumbling Citadel of Kutayha largely dates from the Byzantine era. Here Timur established a headquarters while his armies terrorised western Anatolia as far as Izmir and the Aegean coast. (Author's photograph)

It was also normal for the troops of a defeated foe to be enlisted in the victor's army. Though Timur's tendency towards massacre must have reduced such a pool of recruits, he did welcome those who fought loyally and survived. One paragraph in Timur's 'Institutions', a book of advice addressed to his successors, stated that:

'The enemy soldier, who is firmly loyal to his master, has my friendship. When he passes beneath my banner I reward his merits and his fidelity and have confidence in him. But the soldier who, at the moment of action, fails in his sacred duty and deserts his general, I find him in my eyes the most execrable of men . . .'

Various tales recall the respect for a brave foe that was common among Timurid troops. During a battle against the Mamluk garrison of Aleppo one young Syrian fought with such valour that he was only overpowered after receiving 30 sabre and other blows to his head, not counting wounds to his body. Found among the dead and dying he was then taken before Timur who, according to the Arab chronicler Ibn Taghri Birdi, 'marvelled extremely at his bravery and endurance and, it is said, ordered that he be given medical treatment.'

Entire populations were sometimes recruited, as when a large part of the defeated Qara Qoyunlu 'Black Sheep' Turcomans of eastern Anatolia were sent to Samarqand, there to be ready for an invasion of China. The Turcomans were, of course, Muslims but large numbers of Christian Armenians were also herded off to Transoxania. Most were settled in the cities as artisans or in the countryside as cultivators, gradually losing both their identity and religion. A few may also have served in the army, for there are strangely Armenian weapons and other characteristics in the mysterious *Fatih Album* paintings which are sometimes believed to have been made in early Timurid Transoxania (see illustrations). Troops also came from those rulers who found it advisable to ally themselves with Timur-i-Lenk. The king of Christian Georgia went further and actually converted to Islam. The Qara Qoyunlu were forced into Timurid ranks following their defeat but their rivals, the Aq Qoyunlu 'White Sheep' Turcomans, fought for Timur as allies against the rising Ottomans in Anatolia.

Individual foreigners also served Timur, the

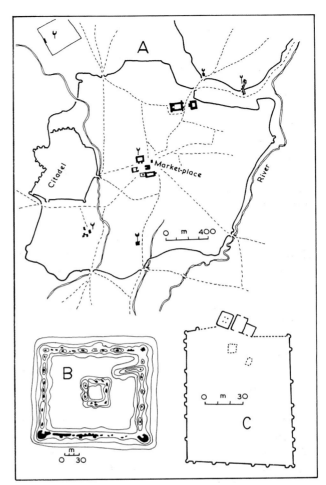

Samarqand in the 15th C. showing Citadel, central market-place and main mosques (after Masson); B—unexcavated site-plan of 12th–13th C. fortress of Kumiyan at Utrar, a base area during some of Timur's campaigns (after Akhishev); C—plan of 14th–15th C. fortress of Zhany Dary in Khwarazm. This region was of major strategic significance during struggles between Timur and the Golden Horde, and later between the Timurids and Uzbegs. (After Tolstov)

best known being a Bavarian squire named Schiltberger. He had been captured by the Ottomans at the battle of Nicopolis in 1396, forced to follow Sultan Bayazit and then captured again by Timur at Ankara in 1402. Schiltberger served Timur-i-Lenk, his son and grandson before escaping back to Germany where he wrote an account of his extraordinary adventures. The Venetian nobleman Niccolo de'Conti arrived at Timur's court from a trading expedition to the Far East and decided to stay for several years, accompanying the conqueror on many campaigns before returning to Venice in 1444. He also described his travels

Among the most mysterious manuscripts in the Topkapi Palace Library are two volumes of the *Fatih Album*, scrapbooks collected by an Ottoman Sultan and including pictures in otherwise unknown styles. Some scholars believe they were painted in Central Asia during Timur's lifetime while others think they were made under the Turcoman rulers of 15th C. Armenia and Azarbayjan. Here two foot-soldiers are armed with curved daggers, sabres, axes, bows and shields while their quivers are of a type not used by horse-archers. (*Fatih Album*, Topkapi Lib., Ms. Haz. 2153, ff.3v–4f, Istanbul)

and could be called the Marco Polo of the 15th century.

Organisation

In general Timur's army was closer to that of Genghis Khan and his Mongol successors than to the armies of 14th century Muslim states. Horse-archers were the most numerous troops in both the central army which always stayed with Timur and in various regional forces. These regional armies answered directly to Timur and could be summoned to battle without reference to local governors. The overall size of Timur's armies varied and, like all medieval forces, is hard to estimate. It was clearly large by 15th century standards and, according to Timur himself, a force he led against

the Golden Horde in 1391 was about 200,000 strong—a not impossible figure despite the logistical problems of the day.

Timur broke the old Jagatai tribal structure into new military formations, primarily to forestall the development of rival power centres. Leadership was entrusted to Timur's own followers or his family and Jagatai forces were gradually settled in newly conquered territory. In addition to units of horse-archers there were infantry forces and, of increasing importance, siege engineers, who could not be recruited from the tribal nomads. Most military terminology remained Mongol or Turkish. *Il* and *ulus* referred to large tribal groups, *tumen* to a similarly large unit of theoretically 10,000 men. *Hazara*, a Persian word for 1,000, seems to have been adopted by both Turks and Mongols well before Timur's time, while smaller formations of from 50 to one thousand men were given the Mongol name of *qoshun*. Like Mongol armies before them, Timurid forces were divided into decimal units, though how far this was reflected in reality is unknown. A corps or sub-section of an *ordu* army was sometimes termed a *fauj*, while auxiliary forces could be known as *hashar*. Such lightly equipped, fast-moving raiders played a leading rôle during Timur's Anatolian campaign. Officer ranks were by no means rigid. Some senior men were known as *sardars*, a Persian word which survived as 'Sirdar' into the 20th century British Imperial Army. Other officers included senior *emirs*, *ming-bashis* in charge of 1,000, *yuz-bashis* leading 100 and *on-bashis* heading ten men. Such a system mirrored that of the Ottomans, both armies drawing upon similar military traditions.

As Timur settled his Jagatai troops, many of their leaders must have been given fiefs which thus drew them into the semi-feudal elite of the Muslim world. Under Timur's successors military fiefs became known as *suyurghal* which clearly had much in common with the existing Islamic *iqta* and later Ottoman *timar* systems. Unlike European feudal fiefs these estates remained the property of the ruler and could be confiscated at any time. Unlike the old *iqta*, however, the *suyurghal* gave its holder control over local administration and justice as well as taxes in return for military service with a specified number of followers. Unlike the *iqta* the Timurid *suyurghal* eventually became hereditary and thus much closer to the European fief. Some *suyurghals* were also enormous, consisting of entire provinces or great cities.

Payment was regular in Timur's army, as were pensions for retired soldiers, all being drawn from provincial revenues. Draft animals and horses could be requisitioned from the people, while various members of the nobility were entrusted with the maintenance and increase of cavalry horse herds. Timur's armies also made considerable use of war elephants. They were not the first Islamic forces to do so but they caused considerable impact by using these massive beasts on various Middle Eastern campaigns. The Spanish envoy Clavijo described the elephants at a wedding festival as having their hides painted red, green and other colours, each with a silk-covered wooden castle on its back; these castles also had flags at each corner, and carried five or six soldiers while a driver rode on the beast's neck. Fighting elephants had curved sword-like blades fastened to their shortened tusks. They were trained to advance in line abreast in a series of short jumps or rushes, cutting upwards and downwards with their tusks at each move.

Enormous military reviews were a major feature of the Timurid army, as they had been since the early days of Islam. Some were organised in Transoxania during the few intervals of peace while others were held deep inside enemy territory. In such cases the reviews were designed to check on an army's discipline and equipment as well as intimidating a foe. In 1391 Timur reviewed his invading army somewhere south of the Ural mountains in the heart of the Golden Horde Khanate. Every division was drawn up behind its

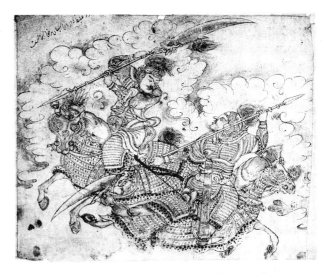

Almost identical to Chinese cavalry are these two horsemen in the *Fatih Album*. Only a Persian inscription and minor details of drawing place the picture in an Islamic context. There is, however, little reason to doubt that Timur's army and those of his eastern foes included such horsemen. Some may even have used these Chinese-style massive double-ended staff-weapons. (*Fatih Album*, Topkapi Lib., Ms. Haz. 2153, f.87r, Istanbul)

tugh or horse-tail standard, Timur inspecting each in turn dressed in full regalia with an ermine headdress topped with a ruby-encrusted golden crown. Every soldier had his spear, mace, dagger, leather-covered shield, bow and quiver of 30 arrows. Many also carried two swords, an ordinary sabre on the left and a shorter weapon on the right; while an elite of heavy cavalry rode armoured horses, some being armed with lassos. The review lasted two days and ended with a mighty roll of kettle-drums and the shouting of the Turkish war-cry— '*Surun*! (Charge!)'. A similar review was held outside Sivas in Anatolia in 1402 before the great battle of Ankara. Here various units were distinguished by having their armour, saddles, quivers, belts, spear-pennons, shields and banners all of red, purple, yellow, white or other such colour. Some historians have assumed that Timur's army was one of the first forces since ancient times to use real uniforms; but the idea had been seen not only in Byzantium but throughout much of the

Some of the mysterious *Fatih Album* miniatures show Chinese costume such as a hat with ear-flaps worn at the top of this picture. Straight swords of a type seen in both Chinese and earlier Central Asian art also appear. But other features, like the military belt and massive mace of the left-hand figure, are typically Islamic. (*Fatih Album*, Topkapi Lib., Ms. Haz. 2153, f.29v, Istanbul)

medieval Islamic world from at least Abbasid times and was still common among the Mamluks.

The marching order of a Timurid army was similarly well organised though perhaps less magnificent. Timur himself normally travelled behind a vanguard of several *tumen* regiments. Next came the bulk of cavalry units, followed by the infantry and a baggage train carrying Timur's mobile court, treasury, armoury, spare uniforms and other equipment. The baggage train was itself protected by large cavalry formations and was followed by the soldiers' families with their own waggons, tents and herds. Some important tents were carried intact aboard huge carts. In camp the men's tents were pitched in regular streets around the royal enclosure. Such encampments resembled regular towns with butchers, cooks, bakers, merchants selling fruit and vegetables, armourers, blacksmiths, coppersmiths and saddlers. Despite

Another miniature in Chinese style is this illustration of a battle between horsemen and infantry. The former fight with spears and tridents, the latter having essentially the same weapons as those carried by foot soldiers in other perhaps early Timurid *Fatih Album* miniatures. (*Fatih Album*, Topkapi Lib., Ms. Haz. 2153, f.77r, Istanbul)

an abundance of bread Timur's troops, or at least the majority of them, apparently preferred rice with their meat. Mobile wooden bath-houses were erected to enable men to attend the *hamam* 'Turkish bath' because, despite the presence of non-Muslims, this was ostensibly an Islamic army unlike the unwashed hordes who followed Genghis Khan. Western visitors were also amazed by the relative sobriety of these mobile military cities, the drunkenness of Timur's court apparently being reserved for particular occasions. They could, however, be very noisy, with all the bustle and animal noises of an Islamic city plus the frequent blaring of trumpets.

Since Timurid attitudes to women owed more to Mongol than to Muslim custom it is not surprising to find mention of female warriors. This caused raised eyebrows among Islamic chroniclers, though it should be remembered that even in the Crusader era women members of the Syrian-Arab elite could don armour in defence of a castle. During his invasion of the Golden Horde Timur ordered women camp followers to put on spare helmets and military gear and to protect the camp

while their menfolk rode in search of the foe. Ahmad Arabshah stated that women actually fought in close combat, while Clavijo referred to a race of mysterious warrior 'Amazons' who, living some 15 days' march from Samarqand, consorted with their neighbours only once a year. They supposedly followed the Greek Christian rite and were subjects of the Chinese Emperor rather than of Timur. Presumably Clavijo's tale echoed the existence of Nestorian Christian Turks in what is now Chinese Central Asia, a people who traditionally permitted their womenfolk equality in both peace and in war.

Relatively little is known about Timurid flags, banners and heraldry. Timur himself used an emblem of three circles reflecting the 'fortunate' celestial conjunction at his birth. Military flags were certainly used to convey messages and orders, as they had long done in Muslim armies. The signal for the pillage of an enemy camp or city was the raising of a black banner over Timur's royal enclosure. A 'pony express' system virtually identical to that used by the Mongols was also employed by the Timurids, with *yam* (Mongol) or *chapar* (Persian) postal stations along the main roads and *elchi* government messengers carrying the ruler's orders to all corners of his empire. The postal stations were placed a day or a half-day's riding apart, some having 200 spare horses kept at constant readiness. Also spaced along these routes were government studs to provide a supply of mounts for the *elchis* and, presumably, the army. The authority of *elchis* to requisition whatever they needed from the local populace was so great that they were feared throughout the empire. People ran away at their approach as if, as Clavijo stated, 'the Devil in person were on their heels'.

Despite conscious imitation of the Mongol empire there was a noticeable decline in Mongol styles of costume during the Timurid era. This was true at court and even in the army, though it was most obvious in Iran. Bulky fashions of essentially Chinese origin were replaced by closer-fitting Iranian garments. Turbans replaced Turco-Mongol caps, which were fast becoming associated with Central Asian 'paganism'. Timur himself did, however, introduce a new pattern of military headgear so that his men could recognise each other. This may have been the fur-trimmed *kalpak*

The decorated portal of Timur's Aq Sarai 'White Palace' at Kish (modern Shakhrisabz) was almost entirely covered with brightly coloured tiles. Their inscriptions and geometric patterns could be seen for miles and proclaimed the power of the conqueror. Timur's palace is now entirely ruined, with only this crumbling monumental gateway standing.

which appeared in Islamic art shortly after his death, based upon a Turcoman style. The bulk of Timur's troops, particularly those of Jagatai origin, still wore their hair in Mongol pigtails. The army remained, in fact, more traditional in its dress than other sections of Timurid society.

Like all the main Middle Eastern armies, Timur's troops underwent rigorous training. Wrestling was already a popular sport and seems to have had much in common with the traditional wrestling still seen in Turkey and Iran. Much more important, however, were vast hunting expeditions organised on the same lines as those introduced to the Islamic world by Genghis Khan's Mongols. Thousands of troops in their proper military units would surround a large tract of territory and then gradually move inwards forcing all the game into a small area where it could be slaughtered. Such hunts took days or even weeks and every move was like a careful military manoeuvre. This not only gave the men practice in archery and other combat skills but, more import-

A new school of detailed and colourful Islamic painting developed under the Timurid dynasty. This manuscript was painted in Yazd two years after Timur's death. It shows a Persian hero slaying a dragon with his animal-headed mace. He has neither armour nor even the double-breasted tunic normally worn by Turco-Mongol warriors. (**Anthology of poems**, Topkapi Lib., Ms. Haz. 796, Istanbul)

antly, tested unit co-ordination, speed of response to orders and communications. No game was allowed to escape and no killing took place before the order was given. Although hunting provided food, as on one particular occasion deep inside Golden Horde territory, great numbers of slain animals were at other times left to rot. This shows that the hunt was primarily a military exercise but also, perhaps, a demonstration of military might.

Personal example by the officer corps and even by Timur himself encouraged a cult of courage within the army. Timur certainly took part in fighting against the Golden Horde until, as the sycophantic *Zafarnamah* biography put it, 'his arrows were all spent, his spear broken, but his sword still brandished'. This seems to have been quite normal for Timur who, earlier in his career, had been challenged to single combat by the ruler of Urganj during his siege of that city. Timur accepted and appeared before the moat calling his opponent's name, but the latter lost his nerve and failed to turn up. Not surprisingly Timur's personal reputation was high among his own men and, in turn, the accounts of Timur's wars are full of tales of extraordinary daring by officers and common soldiers.

Generosity was also expected of a Turkish or Mongol ruler and in this Timur played his part to the full, even in those early days when his fortunes were at a low ebb. In the brief intervals between his later campaigns, Timur ensured that his army was lavishly feasted, fed and entertained. Deeds of heroism were not only celebrated by official poets but were rewarded by promotion or the rank of *tarkhan* 'hero'. This exempted a man from taxation, entitled him to keep the loot he won in war, admitted him to the royal audience without prior appointment, gave him a place of honour on all state occasions and freed him from prosecution until the ninth time he committed a particular crime! Such privileges were inherited by the warrior's family until the seventh generation, while comparable posthumous awards were heaped upon the family of a soldier who died performing feats of heroism.

The fierce discipline seen in Timur's army was firmly based upon Mongol military attitudes, as reflected in the words of an early 14th century soldier who said, 'The Mongol is the slave of his sovereign. He is never free. His sovereign is his benefactor, he does not serve him for money.' Timur's troops were, of course, paid but their dedication seems to have been undiminished. Islam also imposed its own discipline, particularly in religious matters. The fact that Timur's army was excused the midnight prayer after reaching the north of Golden Horde territory where, in midsummer, there was no true night indicates that prayers were otherwise rigorously enforced.

Stern discipline was certainly maintained inside enemy territory, but on those rare occasions when units proved disloyal punishments could be either fierce or mild. A tribal unit which threatened revolt at Khojand in 1376 only had its *ulus* or unit disbanded, the remnants being incorporated into other regiments. Punishment for defeat could be severe if it was felt that the troops were at fault. During Shahrukh's reign one army lost most of its horses during a retreat and was disbanded in humiliation. A perhaps apocryphal story tells how Timur saw a man nodding off to sleep in the saddle during a long march. He muttered, half to himself, that the man should be executed and a few minutes later a stone-faced officer presented the conqueror with the unfortunate soldier's head, whereupon Timur praised God that he enjoyed such unquestioning obedience. Officers gave a personal oath of loyalty and suffered severe punishment for dereliction of duty. A senior commander who showed cowardice in the field would be shaved like a woman, his face painted with rouge, dressed as a woman and made to run barefoot through Samarqand. Even failure in battle could result in an officer having his feet publicly beaten with the *bastinado*. On the other hand few of Timur's foes could claim such stern discipline and as a result their armies rarely matched Timurid forces.

Strategy, Tactics and Siege Warfare

Timur-i-Lenk was an innovator in military affairs as well as being a fine general. He was also regarded as one of the finest chess-players of his day, chess having formed part of a Muslim prince's military training for many centuries. In addition to chess like that played today, Timur used the 'Great Game' with two camels, two giraffes, two sentries, two siege engines and a *wazir* or minister as well as normal chess-pieces. Other versions used oblong and even round boards. How far this influenced Timur's tactics is unclear; but his regiments had separate and distinct assembly areas, while Timur used deceptive routes, rapid marches and the strategy of the indirect approach. He also knew when to retreat and was able to use this as a positive tactic because of the iron discipline of his armies. Various detailed accounts also show Timur's army using matting and even their tents to cross marshes in Iraq. Elsewhere Timurid horsemen would put their bowcases, quivers and scabbards across their backs when obliged to walk.

For centuries the nomads of Central Asia had been pressing against the fertile agricultural land of Transoxania where local armies had developed effective defensive systems. Timur, however, turned the tables by going onto the offensive against the nomadic eastern rump of the Jagatai Khanate. These little-known but highly successful campaigns are among his most amazing military achievements, in which professional Islamic armies penetrated deep into the mountains and steppes of what are now Chinese Central Asia, Soviet Kazakhstan and Khirgizia. The tactic used

by Toqtamish, Khan of the Golden Horde, in the face of Timur's invasion was the traditional Mongol one of drawing the foe ever deeper into barren hostile territory. Timur's army, however, maintained its discipline. It refused to be drawn into ambushes, crossed all obstacles including large rivers, marshes and forests, supplemented its food supply with wide-ranging hunts and eventually trapped Toqtamish with his back against the Volga and Kama Rivers on the northern edge of the Eurasian steppes. Unable to retreat further the Golden Horde army turned at bay, and was thoroughly defeated at the battle of Kunduzcha.

Timur may even have used more sophisticated strategy during his 1399–1404 campaign across Anatolia and the Middle East. Facing Timur were the powerful Ottomans and Mamluks while the Jalayrids had retaken Iraq to his rear. The military historian Sir John Glubb suggests that Timur decided on a rapid thrust into Anatolia to throw

Jael slaying Sisera, from a Georgian Christian manuscript. Though often considered to be 13th C, the arms and armour in this illustration strongly suggest an early 15th C date. If so it would illustrate the equipment of Georgian armies during the Timurid period, a time when Iranian, Turkish and late Byzantine traditions mixed in the Caucasus region (Psalter, Ms. A. 1665, f.205, Manuscript Inst. Academy of Sciences, Tbilisi, USSR).

Most of the isolated miniatures in the *Fatih Albums* are in an identified Islamic style. This battle-scene, probably from a copy of the *Shahnamah*, dates from the early 15th C. and was probably made in Shiraz. The horses have lamellar horse-armour while the warriors wear lamellar cuirasses either over (left) or under (right) scale-lined brigandines. The dismembered figure in the bottom-left corner lies beside a war-drum. (*Fatih Album*, Topkapi Lib., Ms. Haz. 2153, f.102r, Istanbul)

his strongest enemy, the Ottoman Sultan Bayazit, off balance before crushing the Mamluks in Syria and the weaker Jalayrids in Baghdad. Once this was done Timur returned with his full might to settle accounts with Bayazit. Planned or otherwise, this remains one of the most remarkable episodes in medieval military history.

Timur's astonishing grasp of geopolitics is reflected in his diversion of the lucrative east–west trade between Europe and China southwards to flow through his own empire. To achieve this he sacked the Italian Black Sea trading post of Tana on the River Don, virtually obliterated the Golden Horde's Volga cities of Sarai and Astrakhan, and thus smashed the old steppe trading route. Thereafter merchants travelled along a more southerly route through Trabzon and Iran, paying tolls to Timur as they went.

For a man raised in Central Asia, Timur showed a remarkable grasp of naval power. In the 15th century the Amu Darya (Oxus) River, which marked the frontier between Transoxania and the rest of the Muslim world, was linked to the

Caspian Sea by the Uzboy channel. Large boats or barges could use this and substantial ships certainly sailed the Caspian. Timur made use of both during his invasions of northern Iran. At the same time he was fully aware of the wider political situation in the Near and Middle East, seeking an anti-Ottoman alliance with Christian princes in Anatolia and even making contact with Europeans. He was certainly hoping for naval support when he formed an alliance with Byzantine Istanbul (Constantinople), Byzantine Trabzon on the Black Sea Coast and the Genoese trading outposts. Timur did not, however, get the 20 galleys he demanded from Trabzon, nor much help from the other naval powers.

Timur's ability to trick his foes became proverbial. On occasions he would feign sickness in front of foreign ambassadors (vomiting boar's blood, according to a visiting archbishop from Iran). He would have rumours spread that his army was falling apart or would order his troops to scatter in confusion, confident that such disciplined regiments would reassemble at the time and place he ordered. Against a larger foe he would send out small groups of men to light false camp fires across neighbouring hills to make his own army appear larger, or would have horsemen trail branches of

Another miniature from a lost copy of the *Shahnamah* shows a warrior placing the severed head of his foe upon a spear. The victim's helmet lies on the ground and is one of very few representatives of a helmet with a face-mask visor. Comparable but later visored helmets survive and are generally referred to as 'Tartar'. This manuscript dates from the early 15th C. and was probably made in Shiraz. (*Fatih Albums*, Topkapi Lib., Ms. Haz. 2153, f.35r, Istanbul)

trees to raise dust enough for a far greater force. Timur's spy service was terrifying, reportedly having informers among the religious establishments, bazaars and even government ministers of rival states as well as among merchant caravans that criss-crossed the Middle East. Among them were men and women speaking Arabic, Greek and Hebrew—some posing as Jews and quoting the Talmud in Aleppo's main synagogue. An internal police or security force consisted of agents known as *kourtchi* and harsh penalties awaited those mentioned unfavourably in their reports.

The uses of terror

Timur's troops are said to have burned his name into the forests of the Altai Mountains near Mongolia, and Timur himself had a carved stone erected deep in Golden Horde territory to mark his passage—this monument is now displayed in the Hermitage Museum, Leningrad. If Timur is remembered for anything it is for his use of terror as a military or political weapon. He was not alone in trying to have rival rulers assassinated, nor was massacre rare in Middle Eastern warfare following the Mongols' arrival on the scene. But whereas Genghis Khan butchered coldly and with a specific end in view, Timur indulged in acts of apparently pointless sadism. The story that he kept the Ottoman Sultan Bayazit in an iron cage is almost certainly a legend, but Timur did order the extermination or blinding of the entire Muzaffarid princely family so as to remove potential threats to his rule.

At the other extreme Timur's men devastated whole provinces. The effects have clearly been exaggerated but in Sistan, in south-western Afghanistan, an entire agricultural system based upon a fragile irrigation network was so damaged that it has not recovered to this day. The urban civilisation of the Golden Horde along the Volga River was similarly shattered beyond repair. Timur's two sieges of Baghdad put the seal on the decline of that once great city, ruining repairs undertaken since the Mongols captured Baghdad over a century earlier. One of Timur's most savage practices was the erection of towers formed of human heads. Some could still be seen when Clavijo visited Iran, and he described them as being 'tall as the height to which one might cast a

Here the main character, Sultan Iskander, alone wears a full lamellar cuirass, perhaps suggesting that in some parts of early 15th C. Iran lamellar was reserved for the elite. Other soldiers have scale-lined brigandines though their horses carry lamellar defences. (*Anthology of Sultan Iskander*, Shiraz 1410 AD, Gulbenkian Lib., Lisbon)

stone, which were entirely constructed from men's skulls set in clay'. In Sabzawar live captives were cemented between clay and bricks to form 'minarets'. Timur's troops generally carried out such brutal orders without compunction, though when told to wipe out the entire population of Isfahan some soldiers were reluctant to slaughter fellow Muslims. To salve their consciences they bribed less scrupulous colleagues to collect their quota of heads.

Members of unorthodox Muslim groups suffered particularly from Timur's unrestrained policy of massacre. These included the communistic *Hurufi* Shiite Muslims of northern Iran and the similarly Shiite *Ismailis* or 'Assassins'. Non-Muslims suffered even worse, for Timur took no account of the Muslim doctrine of toleration. The story that he ordered his cavalry to ride down a choir of Christian children outside Sivas because he did not like their song is almost certainly a

Eastern wall of the upper court of Herat's Citadel. This was one of the strongest fortresses in eastern Islam and was built for Timur's son Shahrukh early in the 15th C. (Photo Geza Fehervari)

myth; but the way his men slaughtered up to 100,000 Indian prisoners near Delhi on 12 December 1398 is not—though the numbers are exaggerated. Here Muslim prisoners enjoyed the privilege of having their throats cut whereas 'infidel' Hindus were either flayed or burned alive. The Christians of Georgia were massacred in great numbers, while Christian, largely Armenian, soldiers defending Sivas for the Ottomans were buried alive in the moat. At Van similar Christian *sipahi* troops were hurled from the battlements after their city fell, so many being thrown that the last few survived, their fall being broken by the bodies of those who went before. Small wonder that Timur's name struck terror throughout Iran and Iraq, and that the Mamluk government in Cairo accepted Timur's suzerainty after he defeated their forces in Syria.

Tactics

Timur was an excellent battle tactician as well as a strategist. He was credited with new tactics, novel modes of deploying his troops and previously unknown combat formations. He was renowned for making rapid and frequently changing attacks which clearly reflected the excellent discipline and communications within the army. Like the Mongols before him and the Ottomans of his own day, Timur used waggons as field fortifications. This idea had not previously been popular in the Middle East where most transport consisted of pack animals rather than carts. Against the Golden Horde at Kunduzcha in 1391 Timur abandoned traditional Islamic formations of a

centre and two wings. Instead he drew up his troops into seven divisions, the centre and wings each having a vanguard while the centre was also supported by a strong reserve. This enabled him to drive off Toqtamish of the Golden Horde when the latter broke through Timur's left and attacked it from the rear.

Timur adopted a purely defensive formation against the Sultan of Delhi's army at the battle of Delhi in 1398. He drew his troops up on the same hill that the British would hold during the Indian Mutiny four and a half centuries later. Knowing that his men would face large numbers of war elephants, Timur had large barbed caltrops secretly scattered ahead of his position at night so as not to alert the Indians. His main defences consisted of a ditch hidden by brushwood, behind which was a wooden palisade strengthened with large shields or mantlets. Captured water buffaloes were tethered ahead of the lines in the knowledge that only these beasts were large enough to upset the advancing elephants. Detached forces of elite cavalry were also posted on each flank. When the massive Indian army advanced against Timur next day it was almost immediately disrupted by herds of fear-crazed camels and buffaloes with bundles of blazing oil-soaked straw or cotton on their backs. An attack and feigned flight by Timurid cavalry drew the Indian elephants away from the protection of their infantry and into the elaborate defensive array. The Indian cavalry and infantry were then assaulted by Timur's elite horsemen from the flanks. Though hard fought, the battle rapidly turned into a rout and the Sultan of Delhi's men were harried back to the gates of their capital.

Before the battle of Ankara in 1402 Timur again had a formidable encampment erected within a ditch, piled rocks and a palisade. He also had the wells poisoned between himself and the advancing Ottomans. This time Timur arranged his army in eight divisions consisting of a left with its vanguard, a right with its reserve and a centre in two parts, one of which was under Timur himself. His guards formed a separate division slightly to the rear, while the main reserves were stationed between Timur's army and the citadel of Ankara which was still held by an Ottoman garrison. The course of this battle is open to dispute (see MAA

North-western tower of the lower court of Herat Citadel of Herat, the only one to have ceramic tile decoration. A fragment of inscription to the left may, however, suggest that a band of writing originally extended along the neighbouring walls. (Photo Geza Fehervari)

140 *Armies of the Ottoman Turks 1300–1774*), but almost certainly tipped in Timur's favour when a large part of Bayazit's Turcoman auxiliaries changed sides.

So amazing and unchecked were Timur's victories that many suspected him of practising black magic and, despite the official conversion of most of the western steppe nomads to Islam, shamanistic magic rituals were still used. 'Rain stones', pieces of rock believed to have power to change the weather, were reportedly used against Timur in 1365 when his army was defeated in a sea of rain-sodden mud by the eastern Jagatai. In fact Timur's 'weather-luck' let him down on a number of occasions, most notably when his massive army was bogged down in snow on its way to invade China. This time the weather had the last word. Even Timur's iron constitution finally broke, the great conqueror dying in the snowbound provincial palace of Otrar.

Siege warfare

One of the main differences between the armies of Timur and of his predecessor Genghis Khan was Timur's supreme skill in siege warfare. The Mongols had been far better at this than is generally recognised but Timur could draw upon long Islamic as well as Sino-Mongol traditions. In fact infantry, skilled siege engineers, huge numbers of unskilled pioneers as well as 'light troops' and a mobile gendarmerie all played a major rôle in Timur's military organisation.

Despite Transoxania's abundance of fortified cities, the nomads who dominated this area during Timur's youth still objected to their own chiefs erecting castles and thus becoming less reliant on the military power of their own tribesmen. Timur, however, managed to avoid this problem and was soon paying close attention to the building, maintenance, provisioning and garrisoning of fortifications throughout his realm. The vital rôle that castles played in the defence of steppe areas, otherwise dominated by nomadic tribes, showed just how strong Iranian influence was on Timur's military outlook. Some were built on the ruins of Chinese, Uigur or Turkish fortresses, for example on the northern shore of the Issyk Kul lake high in the Tien Shan Mountains, though most were in

Turkish foot soldier of the mid-15th C. He is probably a Turcoman tribal warrior and has much in common with infantrymen in some perhaps early Timurid pictures of the *Fatih Albums*. (ex-F. R. Martin Coll., present whereabouts unknown)

the lowlands. Clavijo, who came from a land of splendid castles, described the fortress of Firuzkuh in the west of Timur's empire as a multi-concentric citadel on an isolated hill, so strong that none could carry it by assault. According to Clavijo there were many good castles dotted about Armenia, where one is known to have been held by a lady who acknowledged Timur as her sovereign.

During Timur's first forays into Iran his army had been unable to take defended cities but by the latter part of his reign his army was famed for the number and power of its siege engines. Fire-throwing *arada* balistas and stone-throwing *manganik* trebuchets were used against Sivas in 1400, local prisoners also being forced to work as pioneers. Elsewhere there was mention of large mantlets of woven wattle to protect Timur's men against the garrison's archers while they attacked the Georgian capital of Tbilisi. The need for a full-scale siege could be avoided if the garrison was lured into the open and then defeated in battle, as happened outside Damascus in 1401. Even here, however, no more than 40 heroic defenders could maintain resistance in the Citadel of Damascus for a further month, despite mining and sapping,

battering rams, stone-throwing engines, Greek Fire and a huge mobile siege tower that Timur's troops sent against the Citadel. The walls were heated with fire then rapidly cooled, it was said, with vinegar so that their stones could be split with hammers. One tower did in fact collapse, killing a number of Timur's Iranian infantry.

The power of late medieval stone-throwing trebuchets was illustrated by an incident when a stone, hurled by the defenders of a Mamluk castle in northern Syria, rolled right into Timur's tent. On another occasion the discipline of Timur's troops enabled him to seize Baghdad by making an assault under the full noonday sun of an Iraqi summer. Most of the 'defenders' lining the city walls were in reality only helmets propped up on sticks. Such a coup de main also shows the quality of Timur's spy network inside Baghdad! Archaeological evidence proves the suddenness with which the Golden Horde capital of Sarai fell to Timur. The invaders had previously fallen upon neighbouring Astrakhan, this time in the depth of winter when the defenders had attempted to build a wall of ice-blocks from the frozen River Volga.

Timur's capture of Izmir on the Aegean coast of Turkey pitted him against some of the best Crusading troops from Europe. Timur's army had already fought Westerners when they captured the Genoese trading post at Kaffa on the northern shore of the Black Sea, but Kaffa had only been protected by a small fortified area near the port. Izmir had recently been strengthened under the direction of Hospitallers from nearby Rhodes. The Crusaders had never taken Izmir's Citadel, which made Timur's task much easier. None the less he used the full range of siege engines, mobile towers, artificial hills of earth from which his men could shoot down into the city, and huge fires to crack the stone walls. Most dramatic of all, a causeway was thrust across the harbour mouth to block reinforcement by sea. Even more remarkable for a Central Asian army, Timur's men had sent fire-boats from the Amu Darya River along the Uzboy

In this Persian miniature of 1436 AD the Macedonian conqueror Alexander the Great appears in his Islamic form as Sikander slaying a dragon with his bull-headed mace. The hero wears normal mid-15th C. Turco-Iranian armour which now includes early mail-and-plate knee and thigh defences. Sikander also has hinged greaves over his shins. (*Zafarnamah* (?), ex-F. R. Martin Coll., present whereabouts unknown)

Channel against the timber sea defences of various Caspian ports.

The question of whether Timur's army used firearms remains unclear. Advanced pyrotechnic technology had been available in Iran and Muslim India throughout the 14th century, while the Mamluks of Egypt had been using cannon since at least the 1360s. The Ottomans may have had guns by the late 14th century and certainly did so shortly after Timur's death, but clear evidence for gunpowder in Timur's arsenal is lacking.

The Later Timurids

Timur's efforts to ensure the succession after his death failed. His army apparently wanted to continue with the invasion of China but instead Timur's own empire drifted into civil war. In fact chaos erupted almost every time one Timurid ruler succeeded another. Some of these men were highly intelligent and very cultured, earning a place in history as patrons of art if not as conquerors. Yet the later Timurids were not without military glory, and the eventual failure of Timur's dynasty owed more to the weak foundations laid by Timur himself than to a lack of ability among his successors.

Timur's son Shahrukh eventually reunified a shrunken empire in 1404 but, though he was a peace-loving man, he still had to fight a whole series of wars against foreign foes, the most dangerous being the revived Qara Qoyunlu Turcomans. On Shahrukh's death the Timurid empire fragmented into a series of family states. Ulugh Beg, Shahrukh's son and nominal successor, based his power on Transoxania rather than eastern Iran as his father had done, and he shared the warlike attitudes of his Turco-Mongol subjects. Yet Ulugh Beg was not a successful warrior, being best remembered for his interest in astronomy and for a huge observatory that he built at Samarqand. Timurid decline grew worse after Ulugh Beg's death and even his most effective successor, Abu Said, suffered a serious defeat at the hands of the Aq Qoyunlu who had in turn replaced the Qara Qoyunlu in western Iran. Fragmentation reached virtual anarchy by the late 15th century; yet even now there were Timurid rulers who could claim a place in history. The most famous was Babar, who ruled eastern Afghanistan after being driven from Transoxania by the uncivilised Uzbegs. He went on to create the long-lived Mogul Empire in India. Yet the most attractive of these last Timurids was Husayn Bayqara, who held Khurasan from 1469 until his death in 1506, a date which also marked the effective end of the Timurid dynasty.

Husayn Bayqara began his career as a mercenary in Timurid civil wars. After becoming ruler of Herat and Khurasan he developed into a notable patron of the arts, but he still had to fight to maintain his precarious throne. Husayn Bayqara also remained something of a sportsman and a keen hunter, a characteristic which caused amusement among the effete aristocracy of the late Timurid world. To the very last these aristocrats

A–C—reconstructed elevation, section and plan of walls of Merv, early 15th C. These were erected for Shahrukh. D–H—fortifications of Bukhara which, though dating from the 16th C., continue styles developed in the Timurid period; F—elevation, plan and section of Shaykh Jalal gate; G–H—elevation and section of a neighbouring wall.

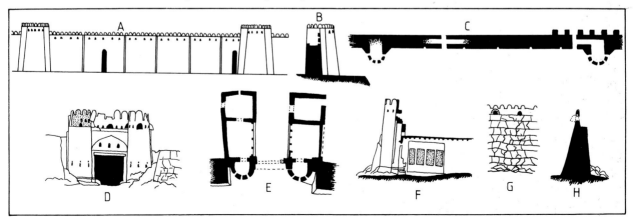

scorned the boorish tribal Uzbegs who were soon to overwhelm them. On the other hand Husayn Bayqara's ability to hold his drink won him the Uzbegs' respect and they often supported him in his quarrels with other members of the Timurid family.

The forces which fought for Timur's successors naturally had much in common with Timur's own army. Yet there were changes during the 15th century. Turks and Turcified Mongols remained the most important troops and came under the command of a *tuvaji divani* or *türk divani*, a kind of general staff which formed part of the council of state. Shahrukh generally left military affairs to these senior officers, and although Ulugh Beg kept stricter control over his army discipline declined by the mid-15th century. Troops of Jagatai Mongol origin retained their distinct identity even in Transoxania, and the rise of the Qara and Aq Qoyunlu Turcomans to the west led to an increase in Turkish military influence in later Timurid armies. Nevertheless the vital importance of siege

warfare ensured a continuing Iranian military influence. This is clearly seen in the decoration of Shahrukh's huge Citadel at Herat which was restored by 7,000 labourers after being virtually demolished by Timur. Siege techniques changed little, as when Shahrukh blockaded Erzinjan with a circle of fortifications just as the Mongols had surrounded Baghdad with a ring of walls in 1258.

The importance of fortified towns in later Timurid defensive policy led some rulers to give *tarkhan* or tax-exempt 'hero' status to entire cities. Large forces were also stationed along the vulnerable northern frontier which faced nomad attack. There are references to beleaguered towns being resupplied with convoys of grain while rebels or invaders controlled the surrounding countryside, and parallels with recent military operations in Afghanistan are quite striking. The later Timurids were, however, forced to withdraw isolated garrisons from their Central Asian frontier although to the very end Husayn Bayqara relied on the static defence of forts to keep the Uzbegs at bay. Yet troops of nomadic Turco-Mongol origin continued to hate towns and large numbers abandoned the later Timurids, many deserting Husayn Bayqara for the Aq Qoyunlu army.

Herat, capital of Shahrukh and strongest city of the 15th C. Timurid Empire. A—Citadel showing upper and lower parts of fortress; B—reconstruction of upper Citadel as seen from wall between upper and lower sections; C—plan of Timurid Herat showing rectangular city plan with the Citadel against northern wall. (After Allen, Bruno and Perbellini)

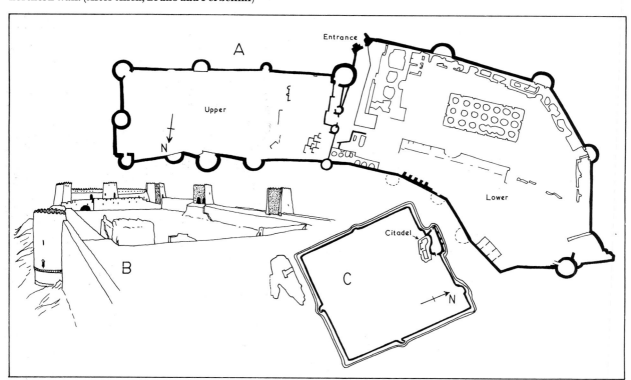

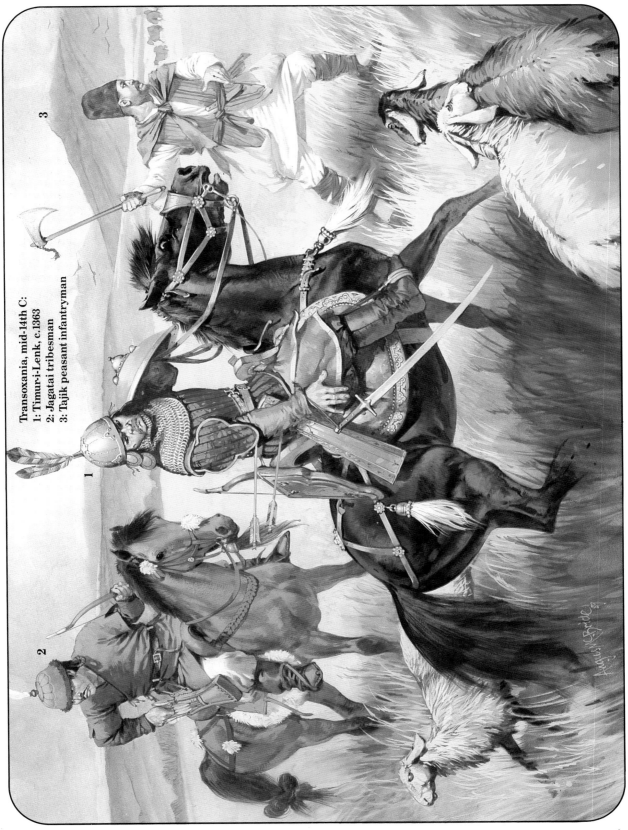

Transoxania, mid-14th C:
1: Timur-i-Lenk, c.1363
2: Jagatai tribesman
3: Tajik peasant infantryman

A

Timur's foes, Iran & Iraq, late 14th C:
1: Jalayrid heavy cavalryman
2: Turcoman tribal warrior
3: Iraqi Arab auxiliary

3

1

2

B

Timur's cavalry, c.1400:
1: Cavalry officer
2: Tarkhan 'hero'
3: Standard-bearer

1

3

2

C

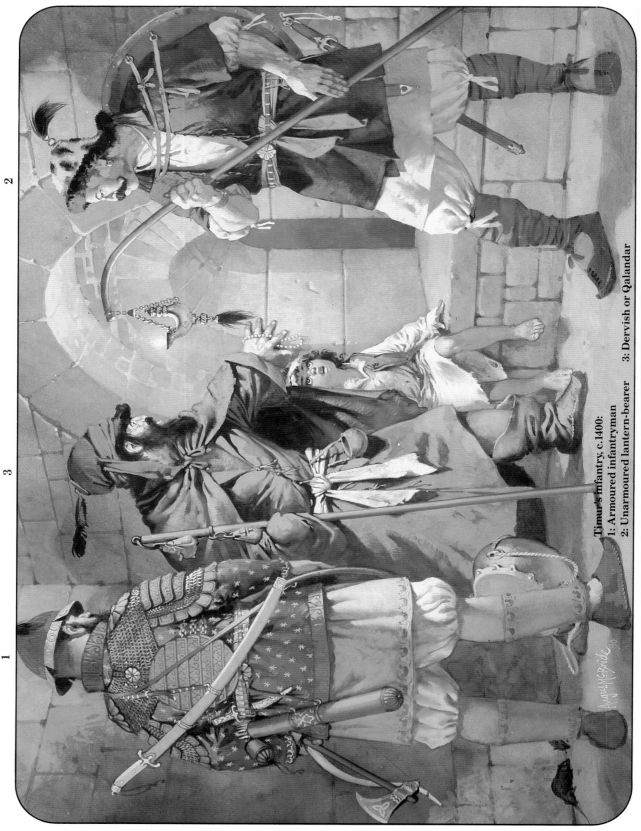

D

Timur's Infantry, c.1400:
1: Armoured infantryman
2: Unarmoured lantern-bearer
3: Dervish or Qalandar

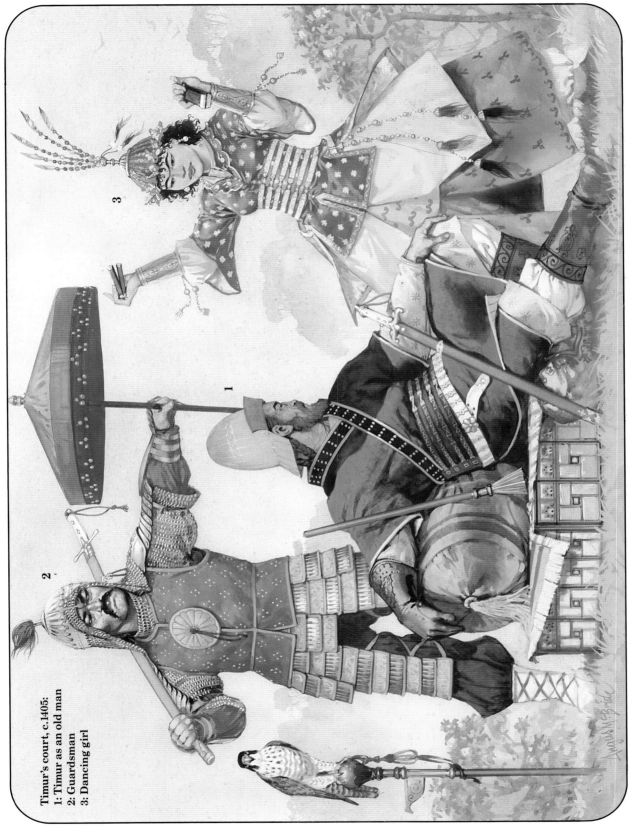

Timur's court, c.1405:
1: Timur as an old man
2: Guardsman
3: Dancing girl

Enemies of the Timurids, 15th C:
1: Turcoman tribesman, 2nd half 15th C
2: Turcoman cavalryman, mid-15th C
3: Georgian cavalryman, late 15th C

F

The Later Timurids:
1: Sultan Husayn Bayqara, 2nd half 15th C
2: Timurid guardsman, mid-15th C
3: Huntsman, mid 15th C

The Fall of the Timurids:
1: Uzbeg warrior, late 15th C
2: Timurid warrior, late 15th C
3,4: Timurid lady and child, late 15th C

H

An increased use of elephants was probably the most obvious change in 15th century Timurid tactics, Shahrukh sending great numbers against the Qara Qoyunlu. They now formed a shock force ahead of each battalion, much as they had long done in India. In fact elephants proved quite successful, particularly in the three-day battle of Alashgird in 1421. Shahrukh's army was also recorded driving herds of camels or oxen ahead of them as they attacked a static foe, presumably so that these frightened beasts would disrupt the enemy's defensive array. In open battle it was still normal for a right wing to form the most important offensive formation, the left adopting a primarily defensive rôle. If defeated in battle a Timurid army would often retreat into the mountains, leaving garrisons to hold the fortifications until the main army could counter-attack.

Cavalry still dominated warfare even in the mountains, a Timurid force being defeated by a similarly mounted Uzbeg army in rough Kazakhstan terrain in 1427. Ulugh Beg's army of 1,000 horsemen plus 20 scouts had routed Jagatai horsemen high in the Tien Shan Mountains two years earlier. During this campaign Ulugh Beg's men had erected at least one *oba* or watch-tower of loose rubble as they marched in search of their foes. Elsewhere they had thrown up a complete fortified encampment because the enemy held surrounding heights, and they also lit numerous additional camp fires to enhance their apparent numbers as Timur had done. Sudden surprise attacks, even against the Mongols who were expert in such warfare, could swing victory in favour of a smaller force. Later Timurid armies still used Central Asian terror tactics by massacring a nomadic foe's menfolk and slaughtering herds so as to weaken a tribe's military potential. Having defeated an enemy in battle Timurid armies also tended to withdraw elite units back to their own heartland, leaving auxiliary troops to complete a conquest or mop up a scattered foe.

Foes of the Timurids

The most powerful foes that Timur faced, the Ottomans and the Mamluks, are covered in other Men-at-Arms titles (see *Armies of the Ottoman Turks 1300–1774* MAA 140, and *The Mamluks* forthcoming). Among others who felt the full weight of Timur's attacks were the armies of a fragmented Iran. The traditional Islamic military system of slave-recruited professional *ghulam* or *mamluk* soldiers had revived in 14th century Iran as Mongol authority was replaced by a series of local dynasties. Urban militias, many based upon *sufi* or 'mystical' Islamic brotherhoods, also played a major rôle. Among them the *sarbadars* (see above) were the most effective. Warlike Afghan and other mountain peoples, most of whom had a long infantry tradition, formed the garrisons of many cities in areas ruled by the Karts. In Iraq and western Iran the Mongol Jalayrids still held sway but their armies seem to have consisted of slave-recruited professionals rather than Turkish or Turco-Mongol tribesmen.

In the mountains of Anatolia Kurdish and Turcoman tribal warriors put up the most persistent resistance to Timur's invasions. The Armenians had by now lost their independence and were caught between Timur and the Qara Qoyunlu

The *Zafarnamah* is an idealised account of Timur's life and in this copy made in Shiraz, 1436 AD, the conqueror is hunting with a hawk. Note the parasol carried by a mounted attendant and the typically Timurid hat with an up-turned brim. (*Zafarnamah*, location unknown)

33

Arms, armour and horse-armour shown in this manuscript from Herat, c.1440 AD, include more lamellar than appears in pictures from western Iran. This could indicate that weaponry was more old-fashioned or remained under strong Central Asian influence in Afghanistan and eastern Iran. (*Shahnamah*, Royal Asiatic Society, Ms. 239, f.206v, London)

Timur's death, developed into major regional powers. The Qara Qoyunlu were overthrown by their Aq Qoyunlu rivals before they could achieve much, but the Aq Qoyunlu went on to carve out a state that stretched almost from the Mediterranean to the Arabian Gulf. They dominated the rich Mesopotamian trade routes, maintained political relations with Muslim states in India and cultivated an alliance with Venice, as both the Aq Qoyunlu and the Venetians feared the fast growing Ottoman Turkish Empire. The Aq Qoyunlu also recognised their need for modern firearms, since the Ottomans were already famed for their gunnery. An attempt was made to obtain artillery from Venice in 1471, via the small Anatolian emirate of Karaman which feared Ottoman

Entire battle-scenes became common in Timurid art, rival armies being arranged in carefully composed groups. Here, in a manuscript of 1475/6 AD, masses of tiny figures include armoured cavalrymen, musicians on horse or camel-back, flags, standards, parasols and a ruler on an elephant. (*Anthology of Nizami's Poems*, Topkapi Lib., Ms. Haz. 762, Istanbul)

Turcomans, while fearing the local Kurds most of all. Georgia was devasted in a series of Timurid invasions and gradually sank into anarchy. Mistrust between the Georgians and Armenians deepened although both were Christian. Georgia was, however, able to maintain close military links with the Byzantine 'Empire' of Trabzon on the Black Sea which remained a small but strategically important state. It is also worth noting that the fall of Istanbul (Byzantine Constantinople) to the Ottoman Turks in 1453 caused less of a stir in the Middle East than in Europe. Meanwhile the Mongol Golden Horde survived Timur's invasions and, though weakened, was still able to crush attempts by some of its Russian vassals to rebel. Interestingly enough the Russian princes generally remained loyal to their Golden Horde overlords rather than siding with Timur's invaders, many of their troops fighting in Mongol armies. The military organisation of the Golden Horde remained essentially the same as that of earlier Mongol states though there was an increasing use of infantry in some areas, particularly in the Crimea, where handguns were reported by 1493.

In the long run the most important and best documented of the Timurids' foes were the Qara and Aq Qoyunlu Turcomans of Azarbayjan and eastern Anatolia. They emerged out of the collapse of Mongol authority in these areas and, after expansion. This seems to have failed; but in 1478 Venetian guns plus 'one hundred artillerymen of experience and capacity' were, according to one record, sent to the Aq Qoyunlu.

The Qara and Aq Qoyunlu states were both based upon Mongol prototypes, as were their armies. Archaic Mongol terms were still in use though the Mongol language had disappeared from western Iran. For example daytime guards were called *turghaq*, night guards being known as *kebte'ül*. The Aq Qoyunlu could also resort to typical Mongol ruthlessness, leaving dead prisoners along their route to demoralise pursuers. The heterogeneous clans who made up the Aq Qoyunlu Turcoman confederation were known as *boy*, the army itself being subdivided along clan divisions. The Aq Qoyunlu army was actually a large and impressive one, with a standing force of 25,000 cavalry and 10,000 infantry to which tribal auxiliaries and allies could be added. Its cavalry were particularly effective, according to the visiting Venetian ambassador Caterino Zeno. One Aq Qoyunlu army of 40,000 men was sent to raid Ottoman territory men but in case of need up to 100,000 could be gathered beneath the ruler's banner.

An almost unique record of an Aq Qoyunlu military review, held in southern Iran in 1476, survives to provide a detailed account of just one provincial Turcoman army at the height of Aq Qoyunlu power. This *Ard-namah* describes a force which included Turcomans plus a smaller number of Kurds and Lurs. Elsewhere Arabs are known to have formed an important part of the Aq Qoyunlu state. A year earlier a Venetian ambassador reported the presence of many foot soldiers in an Aq Qoyunlu army, most apparently being Persians. In the review described in the *Ard-namah* the troops were in three grades: the *pushan-dar* who wore full armour, the ordinary *tirkash-band* horse-archers who formed the bulk of the army, and the *gullughchi* or 'servants' whose rôle remains unclear.

The review itself lasted several days, troops having been summoned from the surrounding districts. Precedence was given to religious leaders and zealots who fought only for the glory of their religion; they, like the soldiers, had their own flags, banners and drums. The parade started at sunrise

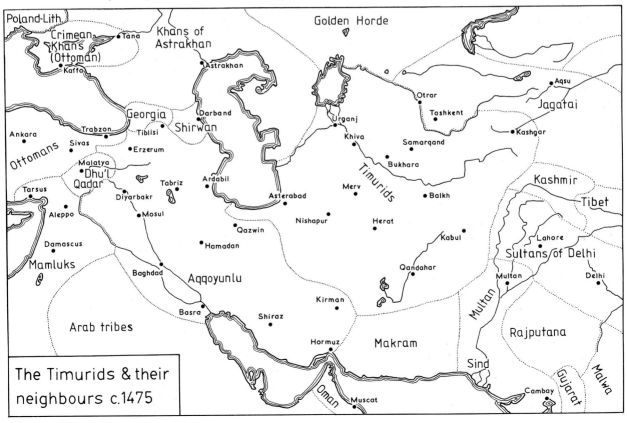

The Timurids & their neighbours c.1475

The late Timurid period was a golden age for Islamic miniature painting. Subjects became increasingly romantic but illustrations of war and carnage were still common. Here, in another battle-scene painted around 1493 AD, turbaned infantry are added to the normal armoured cavalry, drummers and trumpeters. (British Lib., Ms. 25900, f.231v, London)

on a Thursday, passing in front of the ruler who sat upon a jewel-studded throne set on a castle balcony. Around him stood his army commanders, military staff and musicians, with a mounted herald on the ground below ready to introduce dignitaries and officers according to their rank. Military units paraded on the second day, each being summoned in turn by *tavajis* or staff officers who otherwise formed a sort of GHQ. On the right wing was an elite of heavy armoured troopers riding fully armoured horses and led by a white banner. As each unit was inspected its officer prayed upon his prayer mat and then offered gifts to the sultan. The left wing were reviewed next, an elite being armoured though there was no mention of horse-armour, the bulk of troops again being

simple horse-archers. Armoured heavy cavalry seem, in fact, to have formed around 25 per cent of mounted men, though in some formations they were as few as 9 per cent.

Senior men at the sultan's court had their own guards regiments. The sultan's servants, ranging from falconers, messengers and stirrup-holders to kitchen staff, lion keepers and highway guards, plus many other exotic functionaries, also paraded in full military gear. The military engineers or *sanna* were included among these 'servants'. On the third day the entire army drew up in battle formation to be inspected by the sultan who now put on his armour and rode along the ranks beneath a parasol while the royal standard or *sanjaq* fluttered behind.

The hordes of camp followers who accompanied Aq Qoyunlu armies were clearly described by various Venetian visitors. Barbaro stated that the army had 6,000 tents, 20,000 cavalry horses of whom 2,000 were armoured, 42,000 assorted baggage animals, 25,000 horsemen, 3,000 infantry most being archers, 15,000 women and 11,000 children. The camp-followers included cobblers, smiths, saddlers, fletchers, assorted victuallers and apothecaries. Among other military duties that fell to the Aq Qoyunlu after their conquest of southern Iraq was the organisation of an annual *Haj* or Muslim Pilgrimage across the deserts of Arabia to

The art of Turcoman western Iran grew stylised and somewhat crude, military figures being simplified with little variety in their equipment. In this manuscript of c.1480 AD all wear fluted helmets, pendant earflaps, mail *aventails* over their shoulders and relatively plain tunics. In addition to a slightly curved sabre one warrior also holds a large winged mace. (*Khawarnamah*, Museum of Decorative Arts, f.211, Tehran)

Mecca and Medina. Given the anarchic state of central Arabia at this time and the huge numbers of pilgrims who gathered from all over the eastern Islamic world, this was a major military responsibility. A perhaps unexpected rôle that fell to Turcomans who had risen to power in the mountains of Anatolia, far from the sea, was to garrison forts along the Arabian Gulf coast to protect the rich trading links with India. Aq Qoyunlu vessels plied such waters, but whether any could be regarded as warships to suppress the endemic piracy of the Gulf is again unknown. An interesting addition to Turcoman military training was practice against full-sized clay model elephants in anticipation of facing those in Shahrukh's army.

Arms and Armour

The 14th and 15th centuries were a time of transition in Islamic weaponry just as they were in Europe. There had been a great increase in Iranian arms production during the 14th century and standardised weapons were being manufactured on an almost production-line basis. To the north, however, the nomadic peoples of the Eurasian steppe still faced contradictory needs for pasture, which could only be found in the grasslands, and iron which mostly came from the forested mountains. The Central Asian tribes would, in fact, face a serious shortage of iron in the 15th century.

Transoxania had once been regarded as the armoury of the east while the mountains of Central Asia had been very important mining centres. By Timur's time, however, the area had become something of a backwater in terms of production and technology. This, coupled with the immense demands of his large and well equipped army, encouraged Timur to take skilled armourers from the territories he conquered back to his capital of Samarqand. The swordsmiths of Damascus were

the best known, but they are unlikely to have been alone in the enlarged armourers' quarter that grew up near Timur's palace. The Spanish traveller Clavijo witnessed Timur inspecting weaponry made over the previous year, including no less than 3,000 new armours. Other arms were offered by subject rulers, Georgia being famed for its

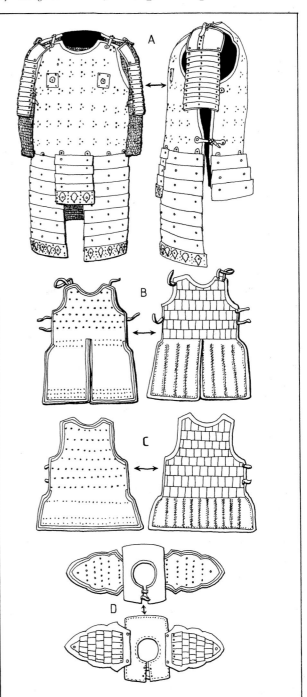

Reconstructions of late 14th century Turco-Iranian armours made by Dr. M. Gorelik and Mr. L. A. Parusnikov of the Academy of Science, Moscow, and now in the Kulikovo Battlefield Museum. Such armours would have been worn in the Golden Horde and by Timur's troops. A—front and side of assembled armour, the front view also showing a mail shirt worn beneath; B–D—exterior and interior views of rear (B), front (C) and shoulder (D) pieces of a second armour.

excellent mail. On the other side of the Caucasus Mountains the regions of Shirvan and Darband had long been famed for arms production and would serve the Aq Qoyunlu as a vital source of weaponry during the 15th century. On a purely technological basis, however, Iraq may have been more advanced than Iranian and other northern centres.

Simple low-domed helmets were the most common form in Timur's day, but bulbous so-called 'turban helmets' had already appeared in Anatolia by the mid-14th century. This distinctive style was not, as is sometimes believed, a Mamluk fashion but may have originated in Turcoman eastern Anatolia and the Caucasus. Turban helmets later spread to Iran in the 15th century and continued to be common in the Ottoman Empire but not in Mamluk Syria or Egypt. Clavijo described the helmets in Timur's armoury as 'round and high, some turning back to a point, while in front a piece comes down to guard the face and nose—which is a plate, two fingers broad, reaching the level of the chin below. This piece can be raised or lowered at will and it serves to ward off a side stroke by a sword.' Helmets with anthropomorphic face-mask visors are more of a problem. They are generally regarded as a 'Tartar' (Turco-Mongol) style but had been seen in eastern Islamic art since 1300 AD—though surviving examples are much later. Helmets generally grew more pointed in the 15th century, some examples being extravagantly tall.

Body armour came in different styles, and different amounts could be worn depending upon circumstances. Relatively light armour would, for example, be used in duels between champions. Once again Clavijo provides a detailed description of some typical styles; this is particularly interesting, as he compares them to well-known European armours of early 15th century Spain. They were, he said, 'of the sort stitched on a backing of red canvas. To our thinking this appeared very well wrought, except that the plates are not thick enough, and they do not here know properly to temper the steel. . . . These suits of scale armour are composed very much as is the custom with us in Spain, but they wear a long skirt made of a material other than that which is scale-armoured and this comes down so as to appear below as might be with us a jerkin.' Clavijo was obviously

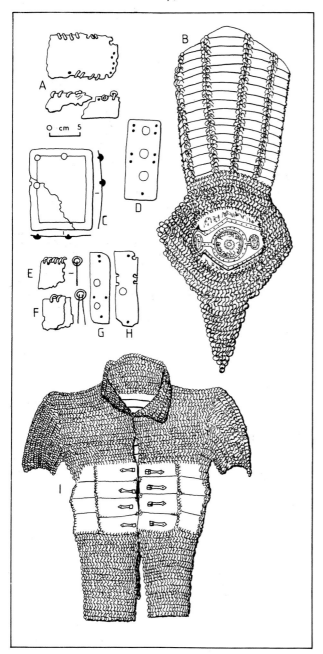

Armour of the Timurid period. A—fragments of mail-and-plate cuirass from Kuban area between the Golden Horde and Timur's Empire, late 14th–early 15th C. (State Historical Museum, inv. no. 341, Moscow); B—mail-and-plate *dizcek* thigh and knee protection, Timurid late 14th–early 15th C. The construction of the knee defence is similar to a European *poleyn* of the same period (Military Museum, inv. 4/3, Istanbul); C–H—fragments of 14th century Turco-Mongol armour of scale (C), lamellar (D, G and H) and mail-and-plate (E and F) construction (ex-Derevyanko and Natsazgdorzh); I—armour of mail-and-plate probably belonging to Sultan Ya'qub of the Aq Qoyunlu, 1478–1490 AD. (Military Museum, inv. 16462, Istanbul)

comparing Timurid armours to the scale-lined *brigandines* of western Europe, a form of armour that might itself have had Eastern origins.

Lamellar armour disappeared from the Middle East during the later 15th century though it survived in Central Asia and Russia. Instead it was replaced by a specifically Islamic form of mail-and-plate armour which was probably invented in Iraq. Here small iron plates were linked to one another and to sheets of mail. This ingenious system gave flexibility, excellent protection and avoided the previous need to wear two armours of lamellar and mail. Mail-and-plate styles continued to evolve during the 15th century, but the *char-aina* ('four mirrors'), in which four large linked pieces of iron protected chest and abdomen, did not appear until the early 16th century.

Venetian accounts describe the Aq Qoyunlu as wearing various sorts of armour; 'Some were covered with strong thick hides [probably buff leather coats like those used by the Mongols] able to save the wearer from any heavy blow. Others were clothed in fine silk with doublets quilted so thickly that they could not be pierced with arrows [either the old Islamic kazaghand lined with mail, or a form of soft armour]. Others had gilt cuirasses and coats of mail with so many weapons of offence and defence that it was a marvel to behold how well and skilfully they bore themselves in arms.' Mail was more popular in Iraq than in Iran, where various forms of padded or quilted 'soft armour' remained in use well into the late 15th century.

Limb defences such as simple greaves and vambraces of iron were known from the mid-14th century and may have been used by the Golden Horde even in the later 13th. New and more sophisticated types of plated limb protections appear to have been developed in the Caucasus and north-western Iran in the 15th century and may have owed something to European influence. Complicated mail-and-plate leg defences appeared early in the 15th century, but hand-protecting extensions to the vambrace were greatly simplified during the same period. Leg armour was, however, abandoned in many parts of Iran and Transoxania by the late 15th century.

Horse armour was widespread and had, of course, been used throughout the Islamic era. Once again, some of the most detailed descriptions

Though stylised, the art of Turcoman western Iran could also be detailed. This manuscript made in Gilan in 1494 AD shows cavalry whose presumably mail or mail-and-plate body armour is unseen under their tunics. The hiding of armour beneath other clothing was a long-established Middle Eastern tradition and appears to have been normal among the 15th C. Ottoman Turks and Egyptian Mamluks as well as the Turcoman Aq Qoyunlu. (*Shahnamah*, location unknown)

come from Venetian visitors. Joseph Barbaro stated that, of the 2,000 armoured cavalry mounts at an Aq Qoyunlu review in 1474, some were 'covered with certain armour of iron made in little squares and wrought with gold and silver, tacked together with small mail which hanged down in manner to the ground, and under the gold it had a fringe. The rest were covered with some leather after our [Venetian] manner, some with silk and some with quilted work so thick that an arrow could not have passed through it.' Such horse-armour was apparently made in the Caucasus region of Kubachi.

Weapons were standardised, though those of the elite could be highly decorated. Large quantities of nephrite jade were brought back to Transoxania by Ulugh Beg's army following its expedition against the Jagatai Mongols. Most was for the decoration of Timur's tomb, but it is interesting to note that many splendid 15th century Trans-

The names of few medieval Islamic artists have survived, but at the close of the Timurid period one great name is preserved. Bihzad ranks with the world's finest painters and although he is best remembered for introducing new subjects such as genuine portraiture, he also painted traditional scenes. Here the guards of one of the last Timurids, Sultan Husayn Bayqara, attend their ruler while he consults a hermit. Note an armoured soldier has the mail *aventail* of his helmet hooked up over his nasal. (British Lib., Ms. Or. 6810, London)

oxanian sabres had fragile and impractical jade quillons. Timur himself wielded a bull-headed mace, a partially symbolic weapon used by Turkish and Iranian chieftains for many centuries. A large number of archer's thumb-rings have been found in Turco-Mongol and other Islamic areas of this period. The use of such thumb-rings was, however, regarded as a sign of weakness though they were useful for long-range shooting. Thumb-rings rarely appear in Persian manuscript painting; but an apparent 'leopard's tail' wrapped around the arrows in some quivers does become common in the 15th century. It may have been to separate different kinds of arrows or could simply have held the arrows steady when riding. The *nawak* or arrow-guide was used in Central Asia as late as the end of the 15th century in defence of a castle. There is also the interesting possibility of crossbows being used in defence of fortified positions at this time. Meanwhile the javelin survived, largely as a hunting weapon.

Further reading

Despite Tamerlane's notoriety and his rôle in such literary masterpieces as Christopher Marlowe's play *Tamberlaine the Great*, Tamerlane has received relatively little serious attention from Western scholars. His descendants, the Timurid dynasty, and their rivals have been even more poorly served. Listed below are general histories which deal with the Timurid period and some more specialised works, many having originally been written in Russia many years ago.

M. M. Alexandrescu-Dersca, *La Campagne de Timur en Anatolie (1402)* (London 1977)

T. Allen, *Timurid Herat* (Wiesbaden 1983)

V. V. Barthold, *Four Studies on the History of Central Asia, vol. II Ulugh-Beg* (reprint Leiden 1963)

V. V. Barthold, *Histoire des Turcs d'Asie Centrale* (reprint Philadelphia 1977)

M. Brion, *Le Mémorial des Siècles: XIV siècle, les hommes, Tamerlan* (Paris 1963)

A. Bruno & G. Perbellini, 'La Fortezza di Herat in Afghanistan', in *Architettura Fortificata, Atti del 1° Congresso Internazionale, Piacenza-Bologna 18–21 Marzo 1976* (Istituto Italiano dei Castelli, Rome 1978)

F-B. Charmoy, *Expédition de Timoûr-i-Lenk (Tamerlan) Contre Toqtamiche* (St. Petersburg 1835, reprint Amsterdam 1975)

Clavijo (trans. G. Le Strange), *Embassy to Tamerlane 1403–1406* (London 1928)

Encyclopedia of Islam (2nd edit.): entries in the volumes so far published include: 'Ak Koyunlu', 'Husayn (Bayqara)', 'Kara Koyunlu', 'al-Kurdj (Georgia)'

H. Hookham, *Tamburlaine the Conqueror* (London 1962)

H. H. Howarth, *History of the Mongols from the 9th to the 19th centuries, Part II The so-called Tartars of Russia and Central Asia* (London 1880, reprint New York n.d.)

Ibn 'Arabshah (trans. J. H. Sanders), *Tamerlane or Timur, the Great Amir* (London 1936)

P. Jackson & L. Lockhart (edits.), *Cambridge History of Iran: vol. 6 The Timurid and Safavid Periods* (Cambridge 1966)

B. F. Manz, *The Rise and Rule of Tamerlane* (forthcoming)

V. Minorsky, 'A Civil and Military Review in Fars in 881/1476', *Bulletin the School of Oriental Studies X/1 (1939)*, pp. 141–178

F. Néve, 'Exposé des Guerres de Tamerlan et de Schah-Rokh', *Memoires couronnés . . . par l'Académie royale . . . de Belgique XI (1860)*

J. M. Smith, *The History of the Sarbadar Dynasty, 1336–1381 AD, and its Sources* (The Hague & Paris 1970)

J. E. Woods, *The Aqquyunlu: Clan, Confederation, Empire* (Minneapolis 1976)

The Plates

A: Transoxania, mid-14th century:

A1: Timur-i-Lenk, c.1363

The young conqueror is shown wearing the light armour of a Turkish prince. His helmet is a simple segmented type with hardened leather ear flaps worn over a mail aventail. His cuirass and arm flaps are of scale-lined construction covered with decorative cloth. He has no other defence apart from his shield, while his heavy woollen double-breasted coat and soft leather riding boots are typical Central Asian Turkish costume. The quiver is also in the Central Asian rather than Middle Eastern tradition as it fully encloses the arrows and has a flap to keep out the weather. The horse's curb bridle, however, is in Iranian style (Main source: isolated page from *Shah-namah* in *Fatih Albums*, Tabriz c.1375, Topkapi Lib., Ms. Haz 2153 ff.22b & 102b. Istanbul).

A2: Jagatai Turco-Mongol tribesman, mid-14th century

In contrast to Timur this man wears no armour and has the simple clothes and riding equipment of a tribal horse-archer. Such basic attire had hardly

Helmets of the 14th and 15th C., showing the variety of styles used by the Timurids and their rivals. They are of basically one-piece construction and indicate the high standard of metallurgy achieved in Islam at this time. A—14th C. Turco-Siberian (ex-Gorelik); B—14th C. Iranian (ex-Gorelik); C—14th C. Turco-West Siberian (ex-Solovyev); D—14th C. Iranian (Wawel Collection, Cracow); E—late 14th–early 15th C. Iranian (Hermitage, Leningrad); F—helmet of 'turban' type inscribed with the name of Sultan Ya'qub of the Aq Qoyunlu, 1478–1490 AD (Met. Museum of Art, Rogers Fund 04.3.211, New York); G—late 15th–early 16th C. Iranian, showing remains of inlaid decoration (Kremlin Museum, inv. 4739, Moscow); H—15th C. Iranian, re-used by Ottomans (Tower Armouries, London); I—late 15th C. Iranian (National Museum, Copenhagen); J—15th C. engraved and silvered helmet with a face-mask in 'Tartar' style. The use of such visored helmets remains a matter of debate. (Kremlin Museum, Moscow)

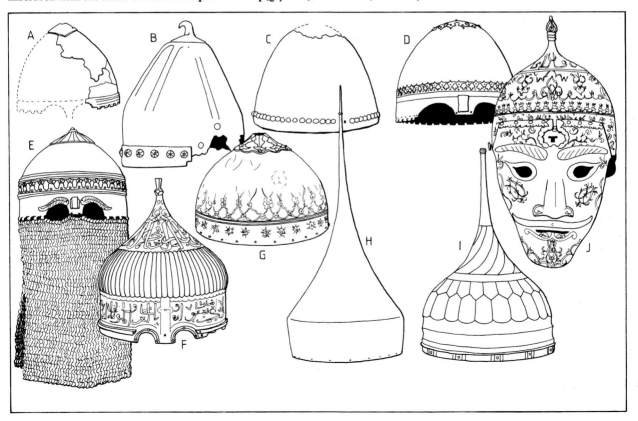

changed over the centuries, but his pointed riding boots and flat-topped fur-lined hat were a later fashion (Main sources: pages from unknown manuscript in *Fatih Albums*, Transoxania or Azarbayjan, late 14th C., Topkapi Lib., Ms. Haz. 2153 ff.23v, 65r & 82v, Istanbul).

A3: *Transoxanian Tajik peasant infantryman, mid-14th century*

The Tajik or Iranian-speaking majority of Transoxania wore different styles of clothing to those worn by their nomadic or aristocratic Turco-Mongol rulers. These fashions had more in common with the dress of the Middle East, though this man's tall felt hat and the shawl around his shoulders mark him as an Iranian rather than an Arab. Substantial 'bearded' axes appear to have been widespread as infantry weapons throughout much of the Islamic world in the 14th and 15th centuries (Main sources: pages from unknown manuscript in *Fatih Albums*, Transoxania or Azarbayjan, late 14th C., Topkapi Lib., Ms. Haz. 2153 ff.3v–4r & 77r; *Khamsa* by Nizami, Baghdad c.1385, British Lib., Ms. Or. 13297 f.16r, London).

B: *Timur's foes, Iran & Iraq, late 14th century:*
B1: *Jalayrid heavy cavalryman, late 14th century*

Lamellar armour was going out of use in the Middle East though it was retained for horses. It was gradually superseded by mail-and-plate, an early form of which is shown here worn by a warrior of the Baghdad-based Jalayrid dynasty. His armour is very sophisticated, including a one-piece decorated helmet with sliding nasal, hinged vambraces to protect his arms and an early type of mail-and-plate protection for his legs. The large medallion-like plate on his chest is a relic from previous Mongol styles while his horse is protected by a full lamellar bard (Main source: *Three Metric Romances* by Khwaju Kirmani, Baghdad c.1396, British Lib., Ms. Add. 18113, f.31v, London).

B2: *Turcoman tribal warrior, eastern Anatolia, late 14th century*

The abundance of mail and lack of lamellar or plate armour worn by this warrior from the Qara or Aq Qoyunlu tribal confederations suggests strong Arab, Mamluk or Ottoman influence. His helmet is of a rather old-fashioned form with ear-

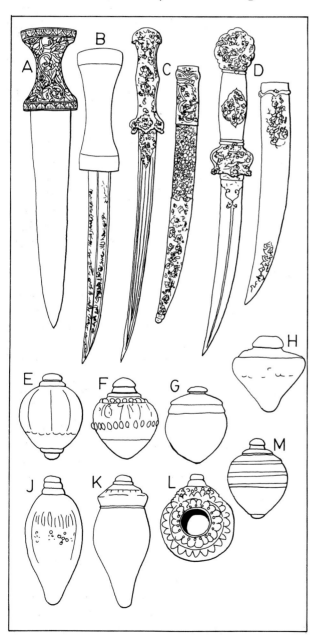

Turco-Iranian daggers and Turco-Mongol ceramic 'Greek Fire' grenades. Such objects represent the extremes of decorated and disposable weapons in Timurid armoury. A—late 14th–early 15th C. Turco-Iranian with gilded and engraved iron grip. Excavated at Osterrode in Prussia, it probably reached Europe during a Tartar invasion of 1410 AD (Osterrode Museum, East Germany); B—early 15th C. Iranian (Historisches Museum, Dresden); C—late 15th C. with gilded steel grip and sheath mounts (Hermitage Museum, Leningrad); D—late 15th C. Iranian with steel grip (formerly in Treasury, Topkapi Palace Museum, Istanbul); E–F—13th–15th C. from Werny Bezirk, Turkestan; G–H—13th–14th C., provenance unknown; J—13th–15th C., provenance unknown; K—13th–15th C. from Tokmak Bezirk, Turkestan; L–M—14th–15th C. from Werny Bezirk. (All grenades in National Historical Museum, Moscow)

flaps and he still has the medallion on his chest, but his plated arm vambraces have an additional flap to protect the back of the hand (Main source: *Garshasp-namah*, western Iran c.1398, British Lib., Ms. Or. 2780, f.213v, London).

B3: *Iraqi Arab auxiliary, late 14th century*
The bedouin Arabs played a vital military though minor political rôle in the Middle East during Timur's invasions, fighting as auxiliaries in both Jalayrid and Mamluk armies. Their costume had changed little since the 12th century and they still preferred to fight in relatively light armour, mostly of mail. In fact this man's curved sabre seems to be his only concession to new military styles of Turco-Mongol origin (Main source: *Three Metric Romances* by Khwaju Kirmani, Baghdad c.1396, British Lib. Ms. Add. 18113, f.56v, London).

Bihzad's influence is also visible in this magnificent hunting scene painted in Herat in 1496/7 AD. The animals are surrounded by a ring of horsemen while other riders cut them down with arrows or a mace and men on foot carry away the carcasses. (*Anthology of Poems* by Mashadi, Topkapi Lib., Ms. Haz. 676, Istanbul)

C: *Timur's Army—the cavalry, c.1400 AD:*
C1: *Cavalry officer*
There seems to have been a Chinese influence on certain aspects of arms, armour and military costume in Transoxania during the early part of the 15th century. This might be reflected in some strange paintings in the *Fatih Albums* (see above). Here a splendidly attired warrior is almost certainly an officer or *tarkhan* 'hero'. His lamellar body armour is covered with embroidered strips of cloth and is worn over a mail hauberk cut away at the rear for ease when riding. His tall helmet is clearly in East Asian style and appears to be of segmented construction, while his sword is straight and double-edged rather than being a curved sabre. Otherwise his weapons are typically Turco-Mongol (Main sources: miniatures from unidentified manuscript in *Fatih Albums*, Transoxania or Azarbayjan, late 14th–early 15th C., Topkapi Lib., Ms. Haz. 2153, f.138v. & Ms. Haz. 2160, f.88r, Istanbul).

C2: *Tarkhan 'hero'*
This man has been given the fullest armour seen in late 14th and early 15th century Iranian eastern Islamic sources. He is obviously prepared for close combat though he still carries archery equipment. The lamellar neck-guard worn over a mail aventail is of Mongol derivation while the anthropomorphic visor is in a so-called 'Tartar' style. He has a scale-lined cuirass over a mail hauberk and his arm, hand, leg and feet defences are very elaborate. The horse's armour is, by contrast, in a style seen throughout Central Asia for centuries (Main sources: miniature from a *Shahnamah*, Azarbayjan, late 14th C., in *Fatih Albums*, Topkapi Lib., Ms. Haz. 2153, ff.35a, 52b–53a & 102a, Istanbul).

C3: *Standard-bearer*
This man's equipment is based upon evidence from the Golden Horde but there is little reason to doubt that comparable arms and armour were used by Turco-Mongol elements in Timur's army. His helmet is an early form of Turkish *chichak* which was in turn the ancestor of 17th century European 'Cromwellian' helmets. The only body armour is a sleeveless scale-lined cuirass with substantial laminated thigh and groin protecting tassets (Main source: M. V. Gorelik, *Medieval Mongolian Arms*, Ulan Bator 1978, & in *The Battle of Kulikova in the History and Culture of our Nation*, Moscow 1983).

D: *Timur's Army—the infantry, c.1400 AD:*
D1: *Armoured infantryman*
Timur's later successes in siege warfare suggest that his infantry must have been good. They appear in a number of pictorial sources, though few wear armour. This man's hat or helmet finds few parallels in the Middle East though there are

Bihzad and many of his followers were transported to western Iran after the fall of the Timurids. There Bihzad produced this portrait of his previous master, Sultan Husayn Bayqara. It was made in the first years of the 16th C. and shows the cultured Timurid prince with a dagger and two pens in his belt. (ex-F. R. Martin Coll., present whereabouts unknown)

echoes in China. His mixed lamellar and mail armour is structurally similar to that of the cavalry (Plate C1) though the large circular piece of apparent lamellar construction which protects his back is a very strange item of armour; it is fastened by hooks and short pieces of chain to a similar piece on his chest. Note that the archery equipment of a foot soldier differs from that of a horseman. He has no bowcase and his quiver is a different form (Main sources: miniatures from unidentified manuscripts in *Fatih Albums*, Transoxania or Azarbayjan, late 14th–early 15th C., Topkapi Lib., Ms. Haz. 2153, f.138v & Ms. Haz. 2160, f.88r, Istanbul).

D2: Unarmoured lantern-bearer

Most infantry had been unarmoured throughout Islamic military history. The only features which distinguish this man are his top-knot hair style, his unusual tunic with a raised semi-stiff collar, his obviously Central Asian fur hat and his sword, which again betrays Chinese influence (Main sources: miniatures from unidentified manuscripts in *Fatih Albums*, Transoxania or Azarbayjan, late 14th–early 15th C., Topkapi Lib., Ms. Haz. 2153, ff.3v–4r, 29v, 77r & Ms. Haz. 2160, f.88r, Istanbul; Mus. of Fine Arts, Ms. 14.542, Boston).

D3: Dervish or Qalandar

Muslim mystics apparently accompanied Timur's armies in considerable numbers. Those from Transoxania often retained certain pre-Islamic 'shamanist' practices. This is reflected in their dress and in the objects they carried, including the drum and staff with small leather bags containing charms, religious scripts and the like (Main sources: illustrations from unidentified manuscripts in *Fatih Albums*, Transoxania or Azarbayjan, late 14th and early 15th C., Ms. Haz. 2153, ff.29v, 38v & 128r, Istanbul).

E: Timur's Court, c.1405 AD:
E1: Timur as an old man

The blood-thirsty conqueror retained his vigour to a great age. Here he is shown wearing the taller cap which came into fashion early in the 15th century. Timur is also prepared for hunting, with a hawking glove on his hand and his favourite bird on an elaborate perch. The multiple belts around his waist seem to have been an aristocratic fashion developed from a waist support used by nomads who spent days in the saddle. Timur's enormous winged mace is largely a ceremonial weapon, while his sword is again straight rather than being a curved sabre (Main sources: illustrations from unidentified manuscripts in *Fatih Albums*, Transoxania or Azerbayjan, late 14th–early 15th C., Topkapi Lib., Ms. Haz. 2153, ff.6v, 47r & Ms. Haz. 2160, f. 51r, Istanbul).

E2: Guardsman

An elite warrior of Timur's personal guard has been given a mixture of Central Asian and Islamic armour. The helmet with its one-piece bowl and mail aventail pulled up over a sliding nasal is essentially Iranian. The laminated upper-arm defences are like those found in the Golden Horde while the lower-arm vambraces are again Islamic. The scale-lined cuirass is worn over a short mail hauberk while the thigh, groin and buttock protections are among the last pieces of lamellar armour to be worn in eastern Islamic lands (Main sources: pages from fragmented *Shahnamahs* in *Fatih Albums*, Iran & Iraq late 14th C., Topkapi Lib., Ms. Haz. 2153, ff.73r & 102v & 105r, Istanbul).

E3: Dancing girl

Female costume at Timur's Court was exceptionally colourful and bore little relation to traditional Islamic values. Many styles, including this girl's basic clothing, obviously owed their origins to long-established Iranian 'private' or harem fashions but others, including the girl's multiple belts and headdress, seem to have been Turkish (Main sources: illustrations from unidentified manuscripts in *Fatih Albums*, Transoxania or Azarbayjan, late

14th–early 15th C., Topkapi Lib., Ms. Haz. 2153, ff.3v–4r, 111v & Ms. Haz. 2160, ff.70v, 77v, Istanbul).

F: Enemies of the Timurids, 15th century:
F1: Turcoman tribesman, second half of 15th century

Fifteenth century Iranian and Anatolian manuscripts show that infantry continued to play an important rôle in warfare, particularly in the mountainous regions of what had been Armenia. Such troops, whether tribesmen or urban militias, had much in common with Timur's infantry and their costumes also reflected residual Byzantine or early Ottoman influence. This man's buttoned tunic may be an example. His weaponry is otherwise typically Turco-Islamic though his quiver is of a form now associated with foot soldiers (Main source: 'Turkish warrior', pen drawing, Iran c.1430, ex-F. R. Martin Coll., present whereabouts unknown).

F2: Turcoman cavalryman, mid-15th century

The cavalry elite of the Turcoman Qara Qoyunlu

Turco-Mongol archery. A—composite bow of late form, unstrung to show weapon curving sharply forward when at rest; B—bow when strung and its main parts with their Persian names; C—composite bow fully drawn, showing much longer pull than was possible with a simple European bow; D—'Mongol' thumb-draw, here using a ring to protect thumb and indicating how string can be pulled back to much sharper angle than possible with the 'Mediterranean' draw used in Europe; E—remains of a probably 14th C. leather bowcase from western Siberia of type used throughout the Turco-Mongol and most of the Islamic worlds (ex-Solovyev); F—archer's bronze thumb-ring with Persian inscription, possibly 1350–1450 AD (City Museums and Art Galleries, Birmingham); G—archer's bronze thumb-ring from Golden Horde mid-13th–early 15th C. (State Hist. Museum, inv. 78067, Moscow)

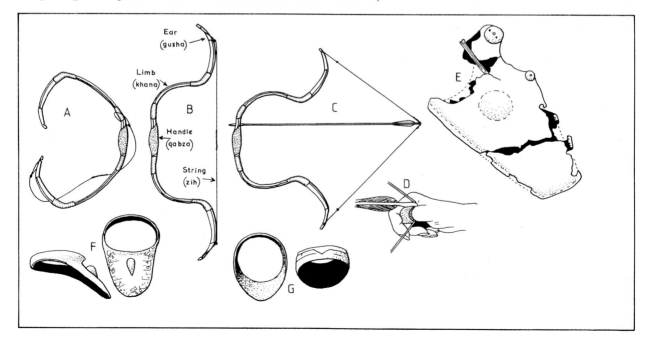

The military fashions as well as artistic styles of the late Timurid period continued into the first years of the subsequent Safavid dynasty. Here, in a manuscript of 1499/1500 AD, horseman and infantry lead a princess and her ladies on a journey. (Topkapi Lib., Ms. Haz. 831, Istanbul)

and Aq Qoyunlu armies appear to have been equipped in a manner closer to that of the rising Ottomans than to the troops of Transoxania. This man wears an early form of so-called 'turban helmet' which may have been developed in eastern Anatolia. Apart from his plated arm vambraces and mail-and-plate leg defences, he is protected by a scale or mail lined tunic. Note that the rivets holding the internal protective layer do not extend below the waist. His horse's armour is of cloth-covered lamellar (Main sources: *Shahnamah*, western Iran mid-15th C., British Lib., Ms. 1948–10–9–50 & 052, London; *Shahnamah*, western Iran mid-15th C., Bodleian Lib., Ms. Add 176, Oxford; helmet & leg armour, late 15th C., Aq Qoyunlu, Askeri Mus., Istanbul).

F3: Georgian cavalryman, late 15th century
Although the Georgians maintained close links

with the Byzantine world, their arms, armour and modes of combat became increasingly Turcified in the 15th century. This trooper carries typical horse-archer's weaponry and is protected by a version of mail-and-plate cuirass that was coming to dominate armour throughout the Ottoman Empire, its Islamic neighbours and even Russia (Main sources: *Psalter*, Georgian, probably 15th C., Manuscript Institute, Ms. A.1665, Tblisi; Turkish or Russian mail-and-plate cuirass, 15th C., Kulikova Battlefield Museum).

G: The Later Timurids:
G1: Sultan Husayn Bayqara of Herat, second half of 15th century
Husayn Bayqara was a successful commander as well as an enthusiastic huntsman. Here he is shown in court costume, which had much in common with that of the early Ottoman empire and clearly showed how Central Asian fashions had been abandoned in favour of traditional Islamic-Iranian styles. The Sultan is using a pellet bow, a weapon reserved for hunting, and carries a substantial knife with which to despatch stunned animals according to Islamic ritual. His other weapons are typical of the 15th century eastern Islamic world (Main source: portrait of Sultan Husayn by Bihzad, c.1500, ex-F. R. Martin Coll., present whereabouts unknown).

G2: Timurid guardsman, mid-15th century
This illustration gives a good impression of the clothes worn beneath armour and heavy Turco-Mongol coats. The man has a broad-brimmed hat to protect him from the sun, carries a bow over his arm suggesting that much of the time he expects to be on foot, and wears voluminous trousers over a short double-breasted shirt. His weapons are otherwise typical of the 15th century eastern Islamic world (Main sources: 'Hunting scene', Timurid c.1460 AD, ex-Imperial Lib., St. Petersburg, present whereabouts unknown; *Shahnamah*, Iran mid-15th C., Museum of Art, Ms. 56.10, Cleveland; *Nizami Poems*, Herat 1445/6 AD, Topkapi Lib., Ms. Haz. 781, Istanbul).

G3: Huntsman, mid-15th century
The humble tribesmen who served as beaters in the enormous hunts organised by Timurid rulers are

usually shown wearing traditional Iranian peasant costume. They are rarely armed with more than a dagger though this man does carry a hefty wooden cudgel (Main source: 'Hunting scene', Timurid c.1460 AD, ex-Imperial Lib., St. Petersburg, present whereabouts unknown).

H: The Fall of the Timurids:
H1: Uzbeg warrior, late 15th century
The Uzbegs were still steppe nomads when they drove the Timurids from Transoxania and completed the Turcification of this region. Though few illustrations survive from their early days, they appear to have used very traditional equipment including lamellar armour and segmented helmets in the Mongol style (Main sources: M. V. Gorelik, *Medieval Mongolian Arms*, Ulan Bator 1978; helmet from Tiraspolski graves, 14th C., location unknown; *Nizami Poems*, Iran mid-15th C., Topkapi Lib., Ms. Haz. 762, Istanbul).

H2: Timurid warrior, late 15th century
This well-equipped cavalryman has been captured and his hand bound to a wooden yoke, as shown in various manuscripts. The quality and style of his helmet, scale cuirass, plated vambraces and mail-and-plate leg armour contrast strongly with the old-fashioned armour of his captor (Main sources: *Zafar-namah*, Herat c.1495 AD, Mus. of Fine Arts, Boston; *Zafar-namah*, Herat c.1495 AD, Pierpont Morgan Lib., New York).

H3 & 4: Timurid lady and child, late 15th century
Traditional Islamic or Iranian styles of costume replaced Turco-Mongol fashions in women's clothing just as they did male costume in the 15th century Timurid realms. Thus this lady's dress comes closer to Islamic ideals of modesty, although 15th century eastern Islamic women still wore very

The rise of the Persian Safavids also spelt doom for the Turcoman Aq Qoyunlu dynasty of Iraq and western Iran. Here the Turcoman Sultan Murad is shown as a prisoner of Shah Ismail in 1502 AD, the year that the Aq Qoyunlu were finally defeated in the great battle of Shurur. (ex-F. R. Martin Coll., present whereabouts unknown)

colourful clothes. Children's clothing, in contrast, appears almost unchanged for a thousand years (Main sources: *Mihr-u Mushari*, Transoxania early 16th C., Freer Gallery, Washington; pen drawings of court ladies by Bihzad & his school, Timurid late 15th–early 16th C., ex-F. R. Martin Coll., present whereabouts unknown).

Notes sur les planches en couleur

A1 Ce jeune guerrier porte l'armure légère d'un prince turc, la cuirasse et les pans des bras de l'armure à écailles sont couverts d'étoffe. Seule la bride de harnais est de style iranien plutôt que caractéristique d'Asie centrale. **A2** Le costume simple d'un archer à cheval sans armure, qui changea à peine pendant des siècles, quoique les bottes à pointes et le chapeau plat doublé de fourrure soient caractéristiques de cette période plus tardive. **A3** Le costume iranien de la plupart de l'infanterie transoxanienne la distinguait de ses souverains nomadiques turco-mongols.

B1 Une armure sophistiquée alliant mailles et plates, telle que la porta ce guerrier de la dynastie établie à Bagdad, remplaçait l'armure lamellée, que son cheval portait encore. **B2** Guerrier de la région Est de l'Anatolie, présentant une influence arabe, mamelouk ou ottomane marquée. **B3** Les bédoins combattirent comme troupes auxiliaires dans les armées de Jalayrid et Mamelouk; ils préféraient en grande partie l'armure de mailles légère, l'épée recourbée étant sa seule concession aux nouveaux styles militaires turco-mongols.

C1 L'on peut discerner l'influence chinois dans certains tableaux qui ont survécu dans les 'albums de Fatih'. Ce chef qui a un équipement splendide porte une armure lamellée sur un haubert à mailles; un haut casque à segments dans un style propre à l'Est asiatique; et une épée droite à double tranchant. **C2** L'armure la plus complète vue sur des documents iraniens datant de la fin du 14ème et du début du 15ème siècles. L'on portait une cuirasse doublée d'écailles sur une cotte de mailles, et la protection de cou à lamelle est un emprunt mongol. **C3** Fondé sur des témoignages de la Horde d'Or, il n'existe aucune raison de douter que les troupes de Timur turco-mongoles portaient ce genre d'accoutrement.

D1 Quelques documents, bien que rares, font état d'infanterie lourde, mais les succès des sièges de Timur prouvent qu'il devait avoir des fantassins équipés d'armures. Notez les pièces étranges, circulaires, sur le dos et la poitrine, reliées par des chaînes agrafées. **D2** Notez la coiffure à petit chignon, la tunique peu courante avec son col relevé, et l'épée de style chinois. **D3** Des influences shamanistes, pré-islamiques, étaient apparentes parmi les nombreux mystiques musulmans qui accompagnèrent les armées de Timur.

E1 Le chapeau haut devint à la mode au début du 15ème siècle. L'ancien conquérant, qui conserva sa vigueur jusqu'à un âge avancé, porte ici un gant pour la chasse au faucon; et les nombreuses ceintures qui semblent avoir été une mode aristocratique parmi les nomades. La masse d'armes est surtout une arme de cérémonie. **E2** Nous avons donné à ce soldat de la Garde d'élite un mélange d'armure islamique et d'Asie centrale. Le casque est iranien, les protections sur le haut des bras viennent de la Horde d'Or, les canons d'avant-bras sont islamiques. La cuirasse doublée d'écailles se porte sur une cotte de mailles courte; tandis que les protections des cuisses et de l'aine figurent parmi les dernières pièces lamellées qui furent portées en territoire islamique, oriental. **E2** Un mélange de styles iranien et turc; d'après les documents d'époque le costume féminin porté à la cour était très exotique.

F1 Equipement caractéristique turco-islamique, et un costume reflétant une influence fin empire byzantin ou début empire ottoman. **F2** Costume de style ottoman, y compris l'un des premiers 'turban-casques'. **F3** Malgré leurs liens étroits avec Byzance, les Géorgiens adoptaient de plus en plus des styles militaires turcs.

G1 Ce costume de cour montre la rapidité avec laquelle les styles d'Asie centrale s'effacèrent devant les influences ottomanes. Le sultan, à la chasse, assomme les animaux avec un arc à sarbacane. **G2** Vêtements portés sous l'armure et lourds manteaux turco-mongols; notez le large chapeau contre le soleil. **G3** Tenue traditionnelle des paysans iraniens portée par ce rabatteur pendant une chasse royale.

H1 Les Uzbegs qui demeuraient d'authentiques nomades de la steppe lorsqu'ils chassèrent les Timurids, semblent avoir utilisé un équipement de style mongol très traditionnel. **H2** Les illustrations des manuscrits présentent les prisonniers les mains attachées à un joug de bois. La qualité et le style de son armure contrastent fortement avec l'aspect de celui qui l'a fait prisonnier. **H3, 4** Les vêtements des femmes et des hommes délaissèrent au 15ème siècle les styles turco-mongol au profit de ceux islamique/iranien dans les royaumes Timurid, bien qu'ils eussent conservé des couleurs relativement fortes. Cependant il semble que le costume traditionnel des enfants ait peu changé pendant de nombreux siècles.

Farbtafeln

A1 Der junge Krieger trägt einen leichten Schutzpanzer eines türkischen Prinzen. Brustharnisch und Armstücke sind schuppenartig aufgebaut und mit Stoff überzogen. Das Zaumzeug entspricht eher iranischem als zentralasiatischem Stil. **A2** Das einfache Gewand—das jahrhundertelang unverändert blieb—eines berittenen Bogenschützen ohne Schutzpanzer. Dennoch sind die spitz zulaufenden Stiefel und die flache, mit Pelz gefütterte Mütze für die spätere Periode kennzeichnend. **A3** Iranisches Gewand, das hauptsächlich von der aserbaidschanischen Infanterie verwendet wurde und sie deutlich von den türkisch-mongolischen Nomadenherrschern unterschied.

B1 Ein moderner Ketten—und Plattenpanzer, der von diesen Kriegern getragen wurde, die einer Bagdader Dynastie angehörten. Hiermit wurde der lamellenartige Schutzpanzer ersetzt, der immer noch an seinem Pferd zu sehen ist. **B2** Ostanatolische Krieger, deren Gewänder starken arabischen, mameluckshen oder osmanischen Einfluß aufweisen. **B3** Die Beduinen waren Zusatzsoldaten, die in den Armeen der Jalayrid und der Mamelucken kämpften. Sie bevorzugten vorwiegend leichte Kettenpan-zerung, und das geschwungene Schwert ist das einzige Indiz für den neuen türkisch-mongolischen Militärstil.

C1 Der chinesische Einfluß ist in einigen noch existierenden Bildern der 'Faith-Alben' zu erkennen. Dieser hervorragend ausgestattete Führer besitzt einen lamellenartigen Schutzpanzer über einem Kettenhemd, einen hohen im ostasiatischen Stil aufgeteilten Helm und ein doppelkantiges Schwert. **C2** Der vollständigste Schutzpanzer, der aus den iranischen Quellen aus dem späten 14. und frühen 15. Jahrhundert entnommen wurde. Ein schuppenartiger Brusthatnisch wurde über der Kettenpanzerung getragen. Der lamellenartige Halsschutz war mongolischen Ursprungs. **C3** Funde von der Goldenen Horde deuten ohne jeden Zweifel darauf hin daß diese Art der Bekleidung von den türkisch-mongolischen Soldaten Timurs getragen wurde.

D1 Dennoch existieren einige sehr seltene Ausrüstungsfunde der schweren Infanterie, obgleich Timurs Erfolg in der Zermürbungskriegsführung beweist, daß er über Fußsoldaten mit Schutzpanzer verfügte. Auffallend sind die eigenartigen kreisförmigen Brust—und Rückenstücke, die durch eingehakte Ketten miteinander verbunden waren. **D2** Zu beachten ist die Frusur, wobei das Haar ovben zusammengeknotet ist, und die ungewöhnliche Tunika mit stehendem Kragen. **D3** Vorislamische schamanistische Einflüsse waren häufig unter den moslemischen Medizinmännern festzustellen, die Timurs Armeen begleiteten.

E1 Die hohe Mütze wurde zu Beginn des 15. Jahrhunderts modern. Der alte Eroberer, der seine Stärke bis ins hohe Alter beibehielt, trägt hier einen Falkenhandschuh. Die zahlreichen Gürtel waren anscheinend eine aristokratische Neugelegenheit unter den Nomaden. Der Streitkolben war hauptsächlich eine Waffe für Zeremonien. **E2** Diesem Elite-Wachmann haben wir eine Mischung aus zentralasiatischer und islamischer Panzerung gegeben. Der Helm ist aus dem Iran, der Oberarmschutz stammte von der Goldenen Horde, und die Armschienen sind islamisch. Der schuppenartige Brustharnisch wurde über einem kurzen Kettenhemd getragen. Schutzbekleidung für Oberschenkel und Unterleib waren die letzten lamellenartigen Ausrüstungsstücke, die in ostislamischen Ländern benutzt wurden. **E2** Eine Mischung aus iranischem und türkischem Stil; die Gewänder der Hofdamen wurden in den Aufzeichnungen als 'exotisch' beschrieben.

F1 Typische türkisch-islamische Ausrüstung, und ein Gewand, das den spät-byzantinischen oder frühen osmanischen Einfluß birgt. **F2** Ein osmanisches Gewand mit frühem 'Turban-Helm'. **F3** Trotz ihrer engen byzantinischen Bindung wurde der militärische Stil der Georgier immer türkischer.

G1 Dieses Hofgewand verdeutlicht wie schnell zentralasiatische Stilrichtungen durch osmanische Einwirkungen beeinflußt wurden. Der Sultan benutzte zur Jagd einen Kugelbogen, um Tiere zu überwältigen. **G2** Kleidungsstücke, die unter dem Schutzpanzer und den schweren türkisch-mongolischen Mänteln getragen wurden. Auffallend ist der weite Sonnenhut. **G3** Die traditionelle Tracht des iranischen Bauern, die von diesem Treiber während der königlichen Jagd getragen wurde.

H1 Die Usbeken waren immer noch Steppennomaden als sie die Timuriden verdrängten. Die Usbeken benutzten scheinbar äußerst traditionelle, mongolische Ausrüstungen. **H2** Manuskriptillustrationen stellen Gefangene dar, deren Hände an ein Holzjoch gefesselt sind. Qualität und Machart seines Schutzpanzers stehen im krassen Gegensatz zum Erscheinungsbild des Mannes, der ihn gefangennimmt. **H3, 4** Männer—und Frauenbekleidung veränderte sich im 15. Jahrhundert des Timuridenreiches von einer türkisch-mongolischen zu einer islamisch-iranischen Tracht. Es bleib jedoch weiterhin sehr farbenfroh. Die traditionelle Kindertracht blieb anscheinend viele Jahrhunderte hindurch nahezu unverändert.